A Shrop

CW01481085

A Shropshire Boy

A P SISLEY

First published 2007 by Real Lives

Ludlow SY8 1BF

A CIP catalogue record for this book is available from the British
Library.

ISBN: 0-9550050-7-8 / 978-0-9550050-7-7

Typeset by Wendy Smith, Hereford

Cartoons by Kevin Flannery

A SHROPSHIRE BOY

The Regimental Band was on parade that day and after the parade was dismissed I got into conversation with a young band member who seemed to be about the same age as myself and he told me it was possible to enlist at the age of fourteen.

Armed with this information I made my way, in some haste, to the local Recruiting Office. After listening to me for some minutes the recruiting sergeant told me to go home and think about what enlistment meant. If I still felt the same in seven days time, I should to present myself to sit the examination for the Army Apprentice School.

The next seven days dragged by, but come the appointed hour, I presented myself at the office where, to my surprise, I found an old school friend waiting to sit the same examination. We both failed our maths paper by only a few marks. But all was not lost. The sergeant informed us that the educational standard we had shown in taking the exam qualified us to enlist in a line regiment. We both agreed that we would like to do that and were told to report the next day when a Medical Board would be in attendance.

We both returned for our physical examination, and all went well until a doctor commented that my big toes turned in towards my other toes and he would therefore only grade me B1 for fitness. This meant I would be acceptable for a cavalry regiment but not the infantry. The sergeant took up my case. I don't know what was said but I was quickly re-graded A1. I'd like to meet that doctor again and tell him how many thousands of miles my feet have carried me, without complaint, since he condemned them.

On completion of our medical the sergeant took us into his office and waited for us to settle down.

'Right Lads,' he said. 'Do you want to join the local regiment – the Befordshire and Hertfordshire?'

We both declined the offer as we wanted to put some distance between ourselves and our home town.

The sergeant consulted a list on his desk. 'I've got two vacancies. One in the Queen's Own Fourth Hussars and one in the King's Shropshire Light Infantry. Who's going where?'

The request took us by surprise and we stood dumbfounded for a few moments.

'Right,' the sergeant went on. 'Who can ride a bicycle?'

As the whole town rode bicycles, I was a somewhat taken aback, but my friend promptly said he could.

The sergeant nodded. 'You're for the Cavalry then, and you,' – looking at me – 'you're for the Infantry!'

Looking back, it was one of the best decisions ever made for me.

We were told to go about our lawful pursuits and await further instructions. About a month had passed when a buff envelope dropped through the letter box ordering me to report. At the time I was working as a warehouse boy for a large electrical cable manufacturer and my boss was none too pleased at the amount of time I was having off to attend the various exams and interviews. I sometimes think he was quite glad when I finally handed in my notice, though he did at least wish me 'Good luck' in my chosen profession.

When the day came, I reported to the Area Recruiting Office

in Cambridge. War time restrictions were still in force, making the journey from Bedford much longer than it be would today (I wonder?), especially as the locomotive was of a type not designed to haul passenger trains over long distances. The carriages were of the non-corridor variety which could lead to problems, especially if you'd taken that extra cup of tea in the station buffet, waiting for the arrival of your train at any time other than stated on the timetable. If you were travelling alone in a compartment, you just hoped the passengers behind had their windows drawn up. If you were not alone, the only hope was to make a quick dash when the train halted in a station and pray your carriage had stopped adjacent to the toilets, then hope you were able to re-join the train before it went on its way. I can assure you many a passenger got left behind in those days.

The carriage windows were covered with a muslin material with the object of preventing injuries from glass fragments if there was an air raid and a bomb blast occurred in the close vicinity. A diamond shaped area was left uncovered in the centre, about 10 inches across, to enable you to see when the train had reached a station. All name plates and sign posts had been removed in case of invasion so you had to rely on the station staff calling out the name, although there was nearly always someone travelling who knew the route and stations thereon.

After a very stop-start journey I presented myself at the designated office where an ancient sergeant took me and others into an inner sanctum, where an equally ancient major asked us all in turn if we understood what we were undertaking when we had taken the oath of allegiance. With our assurance that we did understand, he gave each of us a bible which we held in our right hands, then raised to shoulder level while we repeated the oath.

After this small ceremony I was informed that I had been officially enlisted into the Light Infantry Brigade (King's Shropshire Light Infantry or KSLI) and that I must present myself at the Regimental Depot in Shrewsbury the next day. I was given a railway warrant to cover my journey and returned home to collect such items as I thought I would need at the start of my 'great adventure'.

My father decided that if I was old enough to take the 'King's shilling', I was old enough to take my first serious pint, so together we went down to the Harpers Arms. The landlord knew I was underage to be on licensed premises but when he heard I was enlisting turned a blind eye. After a short time my father suggested we return home on the pretext of my having an early start in the morning.

Back at the house, my father sat me down at the dining table, produced a bottle of whisky from the sideboard cupboard, poured a drink for himself, then proceeded to give me my first ever talk on the Ways of the World, with special emphasis on my being aware of certain types of women who preyed on young soldiers, especially in garrison towns. At the time I didn't take a great deal of notice but on venturing abroad, I discovered exactly what he meant.

A SHROPSHIRE BOY

After a rather restless night, I rose at an early hour with some apprehension that I would miss my train. On reflection, I still cannot understand this as I don't doubt my parents would have made sure I left in plenty of time. I insisted that neither of them accompany me to the station, as I wanted to start this journey alone.

After the final farewells I caught a bus to St John's station. When I arrived I found I had time to spare so I decided to buy some sweets from a newsagent's just outside the station. While doing this, I spotted my mother trying to hide around the other side of the station. Obviously she had caught the next bus but didn't wish to upset me in any way. I didn't approach her and, to this day, I wonder if I did the right thing.

The train that was to carry me off on my new adventure arrived and took me to Bletchley Junction, where I changed to another train going via Crewe. It was at Bletchley that I learned it would have been better if I had started my journey from Midland Road station in Bedford as I could have caught an express to Northampton which would have got me into Shrewsbury hours ahead of the time specified. Oh well, we live and learn.

My journey took me through Stafford where a large number of recently de-mobbed airmen boarded the train. Needless to say they were in very high spirits and rather boisterous. After they had settled in one of them asked me where I was bound. In my enthusiasm I told him I was on my way to join the Army. He was not particularly interested until I told him it was on a regular engagement, at which, he turned to one of the others with a sardonic grin.

'Have you got a rusty razor blade?' he asked.

'What do you want that for?' his friend returned.

'I'm going to give it to this lad so he can cut his throat and if he doesn't die from loss of blood he could die of blood poisoning!'

As I was new to the 'Army Game', I had followed the itinerary given to me at the time of my enlistment, which meant that I arrived in Shrewsbury after 16:30hrs, therefore outside the normal working hours as far as the Army was concerned. I did what I thought was the right thing and reported to RTO (Railway Transport Officer) in the hope of obtaining transport.

The RTO telephoned the Depot and I was informed that transport to take me there would arrive 'eventually'. Some time later a 15 cwt truck arrived with a somewhat disgruntled driver who was expecting to pick up at least a Commissioned Officer not some fresh faced kid – 'who could have caught a bus from the market place,' (if I'd known where it was.)

During the journey I learned the main reason for his griping was the fact that he had been called from his tea, which in his eyes was a cardinal sin. At the main gates of the Depot at Copthorne Barracks, the driver stopped at the Guard Room and indicated that I was to alight from the vehicle and report in.

As I climbed down, one of the first things to catch my eye was the statue of an eagle, in front of which I was to see many a defaulter paraded, though I wonder how many of them knew the story of the Minden Eagle.

I later learned that it had been 'borrowed' by some young officers during the Regiment's occupation of Germany after the First World War. It mysteriously turned up at Copthorne, where it remained until the formation of the present day Light Infantry. After that, it disappeared for some time until it was offered back to the new occupants, who mounted it on a plinth where it stands today, overlooking the square.

Entering the Guard Room for the first time, I was greeted by a rich, Irish voice which many a new soldier got to know in a very short space of time. This distinctive voice belonged to Provost Sergeant Paddy Ryan, who, despite a very large and robust appearance, would never see anyone head for trouble if he could prevent it.

He asked what I was doing in his Guard Room? When I told him, he instructed one of the Regimental Police to escort me and to see that I was bedded down in the Boys' Hut. In the hut I was introduced to the lance-corporal in charge of boys, as well as to the boys already in occupation. I was asked if I'd eaten.

When I said 'no', I was instructed to borrow some eating irons - knife, fork and spoon plus china mug. The lance-corporal took me to the cook house where, because I was late I was rather grudgingly given a piece of tepid Welsh rarebit, bread, butter, and a mug of tea At this time there was no such things as 'Trays Messing' and as I had not yet been issued with my own mess tins, I was more than grateful for the assistance of the lance-corporal in carrying my food over to the Boys' Table.

The Boys' Table consisted of two 6ft tables, GS, placed together, thereby making a 6ft square table. To sit on, 6ft forms, GS, were placed along each side. All would be well unless you happened to be seated on the extreme ends of the forms. If everyone decided at the end of their meal to stand at the same time, many a young man has ended up in an undignified heap, especially if the boys were in a playful mood.

The Boys' Table existed because boys were only allowed to associate with men while under supervision. This rule came about through years of experience, and as one grew older, the wisdom behind this ruling became apparent. Men were not allowed to enter billets occupied by boys, nor were they allowed to sit at tables designated for their use. Many a newly recruited soldier was turned away from what he saw as a vacant space at a table. Some didn't take too kindly to being told to 'Go away!' At meal times we would be taken to the head of the queue which would lead to much verbal comment, until stopped by an NCO.

After tea I was taken to HQ Company Stores where because I was late (and, judging by the way he was dressed, the store-man was waiting to 'walk out'), I was hastily issued with:

Blankets [3]

Biscuits [3]

(30" x 30" x 4" canvas pads filled with horse hair)

Mugs china [1]

At this point I was introduced to a system with which I

never concurred. It went something like this. If you broke the mug you had been issued with, you would be given another, on payment for the one you had broken, also for the one you had received as replacement. If you then broke the replacement, you went through the system again. And so on, ad infinitum. I never heard of anyone trying to stop this nice little earner.

On returning to the Boys' Hut, I started to learn the first principal of a soldier's life: wherever you go, always look to making your life as comfortable as possible.

I'd been allocated a bed space, a bed [retractable] and a foot locker [wooden]. Then I took part in a minor wrestling match between the bed [retractable] and myself. The bed had an iron frame, the bottom half of which slid back into the upper part, so when you had 'made up' your bed in the morning, it gave more space to the centre of the hut. I have often thought this had little to do with more space more to do with stopping you having a kip during the lunch break

When closed, the bed measured c. 3½' long by 3' wide. When extended (after 16:30 hrs) it opened out to 7' long, providing a good base for the biscuits The next lesson I learned was how to make the best use of blankets, not only in providing warmth but also in avoiding a battle to prevent your hips coming in to contact with the bed springs, if your biscuits came apart during the night.

When it was time to go to bed on the first night, I must admit that undressing in the same room as other boys did take some getting used to, although having belonged to an organisation like the Army Cadets and going to camp did help.

After a fairly good night's sleep I was aroused by the time honoured shout: 'Get your feet on the floor!'

As the hut floor was made of very rough wood, getting one's feet on it was a task to be undertaken with a certain amount of caution. It was amazing the various ways that some found to beat the system. I've seen men sitting bolt upright on the edge of their beds, with both feet on the floor, and still fast asleep!

After making up my bed in the required fashion, ie: with two blankets folded lengthways, then folded crossways at least three times, so as to present a nice clean edge, then placed one on top of the other. The third blanket was folded lengthways then wrapped around the other two. This bundle was placed on top of your already stacked biscuits (on top of your bed frame, retracted). To finish off the picture you placed your knife, fork and spoon plus mug (all spotless) on top. After a wash (I didn't shave in those days, although the time wasn't far off), I joined the others in carrying out such tasks as were required to get the hut ready for the day.

As we finished, we were told to parade outside. The lance-corporal marched us to the cookhouse where we underwent the verbal barrage I have already described as we were handed our breakfast and made our way to the Boys' Table.

At this point I was introduced to 'Dippers'. To indulge in this, you obtained a slice of bread (two if you were really hungry), proceeded to the hot plate from which the breakfasts were being served and asked permission from the NCO in charge if you could dip your bread in the residual fat in the cooking tray in which the bacon or sausage had been cooked. At this time trays (GS) measured c. 3' square and 1½" deep, so there was usually plenty of fat for Dippers.

I often wonder what the dieticians of today would have to say. I expect they would throw their arms to the heavens, but one must remember that in those days the meat was good honest meat, untainted by additives of any kind. Most times we were lucky in our quest and I can only remember one occasion when we were refused. This time, one of the boys had upset the NCO during mid-morning break the day before. It's amazing how one chance remark can upset the normal running of someone else's day.

After breakfast we made our way back to our billet where upon his return our lance-corporal told me to carry out various tasks, after which I was to take a walk around the depot to familiarise myself with the lay out of the place. It was during this exploration that I learned another golden rule. Without giving it a thought, I'd strayed on to the Parade Square. Almost immediately there was a roar from the direction of The Manse – the residence of the Regimental Sergeant Major.

I was ordered to stand still, exactly where I was, which I did, to be joined seconds later by the illustrious gentleman himself.

'What exactly do you think you're doing?' he enquired.

As I was still in civilian clothes I could only tell the truth.

'This square,' the RSM replied, 'is sacred territory and it's all mine. If God wants to walk on it, he has to ask my permission first. The only time you are allowed on here is by my invitation.

Do you understand?'

Satisfied with my eager confirmation that I did understand, he dismissed me. I'm sure there was a twinkle in his eye but I realised that my first brush with authority had not been a resounding success.

Bearing this experience in mind, I made my way back to my billet. After talking with one of the other boys about routines and such like for half an hour it was time for mid-morning break. As boys were so poorly paid their mid-morning snack was provided by the cookhouse. Each of us received one pint of milk, plus bread, butter and jam. As the number of boys enlisting increased so did the amount provided.

At one time the butter and jam was issued in 7 lb tins. It came to the point where, if there was enough of either left at the end of the break, we would ask for it to be kept for the next day. Nine times out of ten there would be a different cook on duty the next day and he would provide not only the opened tin but also a new one. We learned to manoeuvre things round so that occasionally there would be an unopened tin which would find a safe home with one of the boys when he went home. It certainly helped eke out someone's rations.

After the break I was taken to the Band Stores, where I was introduced to the Bandmaster who, although staying in the depot, was actually Bandmaster of the 2nd Battalion Band, which at this time was stationed in Cove, Hampshire while the rest of the Battalion was in Cyprus, trying to deal with large numbers of Jews wanting to get to Palestine (before the State of Israel had been created).

The Bandmaster had started his career in a cavalry regiment and during the First World War had been trumpeter to Field Marshal Earl Haigh. When the war ended, he had entered the Royal Military School of Music at Kneller Hall, passing out as WO1 (Bandmaster) and took up duties with the 2nd Battalion, KSLI. During the 2nd World War, he took over the position of Army Post Master, as he was now classified as non-combatant.

He had quite a chuckle when I related how I came to be chosen for the regiment. I always found him a fair man, determined to teach us all there was to learn in our chosen profession. This was quite an undertaking when you consider very few of us knew anything about music prior to our enlistment.

The Bandmaster took me across to meet the Band President for instruction on what was expected of boys enlisting in the regiment. As I entered the BP's office I noticed he was wearing a very large hearing aid, which we all soon learned had batteries that didn't last too long. All went well until he told me to speak up while he fiddled with a box attached to his belt.

I repeated what I had said, at which he suddenly glared at me and barked, 'There's no need to shout boy!'

I think most of the boys went through this type of interview and none of us ever discovered exactly what level of decibel was required.

After this interview I was taken to the Orderly Room where I handed in my Ration book, Identity Card, and Certificate of Service in the Army Cadets. In exchange I was given my

Regimental Number and 'Demob Group No 76 DR (Deferred Regular)'. This number for 'demob' meant little to me at the time but, as will be seen, later on it did hit home rather hard.

The regimental number was issued in line with the block relevant to the KSLI, as shown in the Army List at that time. During the past war it had been revealed that the Germans gleaned quite a lot of information from 'Number, rank and name', as required if captured by the enemy, so 'non-descriptive' numbers were issued, presumably at random. I don't know why we were given our particular numbers. Boys enlisting about twelve months later were given numbers out of the 'normal' run of numbers, and the RAF took over numbers starting 404.

Necessary details were entered in my Army Book 64, Pt One. These included medical category, personal details, such as disfigurement, height and educational qualifications. All details regarding pay were held in AB64, Pt Two, which I always considered the more important of the two.

I was taken up to the Quartermaster's store, then situated in the Keep, clutching in my sweaty palm a piece of paper upon which was printed my newly acquired number. I was desperately trying to commit it to memory as I wanted to give the impression that I was at least capable of remembering such a small detail as my number. (Today, like anyone who ever served in the Forces, I can recite my number at the drop of a hat.)

During the walk to the Stores one of the older boys joined us as he wanted to change a pair of boots if he could. He told me that not so long ago Fire Watch Sentries were posted on the roof of the Keep, in case any enemy aircraft had the audacity to drop incendiary bombs in the area. I was also led to believe that the sentries had a Bren gun with which to engage the enemy, though how they could have engaged the enemy and watched for the fall of bombs at the same time was beyond me.

Once in the Keep, I climbed the stone steps to the first floor which was the domain of one Private Nick Carter. Nick had enlisted in the regiment around the time of the Boer War and remained a private ever since, thereby gaining the status of the longest serving, and oldest private in the British Army at the time He had a great number of Good Conduct stripes upon the left sleeve of both his Service Dress and Battle Dress. Rumour had it that he never pressed the left sleeve of any uniform.

Good Conduct stripes were awarded on the following basis: One for two years; two for five years; three for nine years; four for twelve, then one for every additional three years. As Nick had enlisted in 1898, one can gather how many he wore. He was the only private soldier in the depot who still wore Service Dress, which had generally been withdrawn in 1940. He always wore it out of barracks and following the same pattern every working day, summer or winter, at 16:00 hrs Nick would leave the stores carrying his Service Dress over his arm. Passing through the cook house, where he collected a mug of tea and a sandwich, he would make his way to his billet in HQ Company lines. After drinking his tea he would wash and shave then have a nap. When he rose, he would get dressed, leave the Barracks, and proceed down the hill into Frankwell, calling at various hostelries before returning to the Barracks at 22:00 hrs.

I doubt if there were any watering holes where he had to pay. When Nick finally had to retire, he was presented with a gilded parchment, outlining his service, which was encased in a beautifully carved casket. Unfortunately Nick did not live too long after this so didn't enjoy the benefit of a lengthy retirement, and it was 'Farewell' to another of life's unique characters.

In the stores, I was issued with the standard kit, less webbing equipment:

Blouses, Battle Dress	2	Shoes, Canvas, pairs	1
Trousers, Battle Dress	2	Boots Ammunition pairs	2
Underpants, Woollen, pairs	2	Shoes, Canvas, pairs	1
Shorts, PT, pairs	2	Vests, PT	2
Socks, Woollen, pairs	3	Brush, Shaving	1
Brush, Polishing	1	Housewife [complete]	1
Holdall, Canvas	1	Razor, Safety	1
Badge, Cap, Regimental	1	Bag, Kit, canvas	1
Coat, Great	1	Berets, GS	2

After signing for all these items on my newly acquired Army Form 1157, packing them in my kit bag, or at least, as much as it would take, I made my way back to my billet where I spent the greater part of the day ironing, polishing, folding and stowing away. I was given considerable help by those boys who'd been in the regiment some days longer than I had. When I'd finished I felt things were beginning to come together.

The foot locker was approximately 2½' wide, 2' deep and 2' high. There was obviously no way I could get all my kit into this container. However, on the wall behind my bed space there was a board screwed flat to the wall from which protruded four wooden pegs about 6" long. Above this was a shelf, 3' wide and 18" deep. I was shown how to fold and stack on this shelf such items as my pullover, spare shirt, and kit bag and to place my best pair of boots, one either side, so that they could be seen without too much effort. My greatcoat was hung by its shoulder straps from the wooden pegs. After hanging, I buttoned up the coat. The back belt was bought round to the front and two of the three buttons fastened, thereby creating a waist any girl would have been proud of.

The item described as "Housewife [complete]" was a cotton pouch c4½" by 5", which fastened down to c2½" and was generally referred to as a 'Hussif'. It contained cotton and needles, both sewing and darning, wool (grey) and a patch of khaki material. Later issues were of a waterproof material, the patch of which came in handy for repairing torn ponchos. All in all, a very handy part item of one's kit.

As in all walks of life, there were rogues among the ranks of the KSLI. To lessen the chances of thievery, every item of your kit was marked with your number. All items made of material such as cotton or canvas were marked using rubber stamps and indelible ink from a pad, while metal objects were marked using metal punches. Even the shank of one's cap badge was marked. I learned that a Boot, ammunition, made a serviceable hammer.

At this point, I was told the 'Golden' rule. If ever a soldier found himself needing to replace a lost item, such as a broom or bucket or similar, he never 'borrowed' from his own squad, platoon or company.

I was also given some very useful advice on preparing my uniform As it was not always enough to cover the springs or possible to have the use of a pressing iron, what better weight and heat than the human body? The method required a fairly large cardboard box, nearly always available from the rear of the NAAFI, or any one of the stores buildings. You flattened or stripped down the box then placed a large piece in the bed (making sure it could be folded so as not to show when your bed was made up for inspection in the mornings). You placed a pair of trousers on this piece then placed smaller pieces between the legs of the trousers, then a larger piece over the whole (again making sure it didn't show).

I found using pieces that fitted the frame when retracted were much easier to push out of sight when the need arose. Some soldiers used this method to press their Battle Dress blouses. However if you were too enthusiastic you could finish up with quite a heap which would give a very disturbed night's sleep.

Boys had to stand by their beds at 21:00 hrs, with kit ready for the next day (except on the nights they were allowed out), laid out for inspection on top of your foot locker. On some occasions this inspection was carried out by the Company Orderly Corporals, some of whom didn't take too kindly to this extra duty and would find something to make the boys' life a little more difficult.

As the days went by so one learned the 'wrinkles', on how to bring kit up to the required standard, especially boots. Boots, Ammunition, have always played a large part in a soldier's life, for rarely a day went by when boots were not worn, polished, inspected or worked upon. When you were first issued with your kit you received two pairs and there started the influence they would have on the rest of your life as a soldier.

Firstly you had to select the pair to be designated as 'Best'. This pair received the most attention – or 'bull' – and you protected them from every possible danger, dreading the day when you had to hand them in for repair. I'm convinced the store-man or the cobblers achieved some sort of sadistic pleasure in handling these boots in the worst possible way, if the damage done was anything to go by. Many hours were spent repairing a scarred or slashed toecap or heel.

We soon discovered there was more than one way to achieve the required standard. One boy would use the heated handle of a spoon, while another would risk burning the stitching of the boot by applying a very thick layer of boot polish, then setting light to it in an attempt to get rid of the grease in the leather. Another would use melted beeswax to fill in the blemishes of the leather's surface.

Many hours were spent working on both pairs of boots but with the greater time being spent on the 'best'. People have often talked of 'bull shine'. Some say this method was a waste of time, but over the years it has been used to give idle hands some work. I often found that a lot of 'bull' came not to order, but from the men themselves. That's to say, as well as achieving the required shine on both toe and heel cap, some would go a step further and flatten the eyelets of the lace holes then polish the result while others would 'bull' the instep These extra items looked very nice on inspection but could cause bad feelings when every one was informed that this is what those in command wanted to see from everyone.

As boys were not issued at this time with webbing equipment, they had little brass to polish. Nevertheless, any deficiency in this area was made up for by the great attention we paid to our cap badges, both back and front, also to the buckles of our gaiters. The straps of the gaiters also required attention, soon making up any shortfall in cleaning webbing.

After a few days it was decided that enough time had been spent on getting our kit in order. We were paraded and taken to the Band Stores to be allocated our various musical instruments, in my case, a French horn and an Adkins tutor. I was then told to find either a quiet corner or another French Horn player and see how I got on. I persevered but made little noticeable progress, at least as far as the Adkins tutor was concerned. I was once told that when Major Adkins was Director of Music at Kneller Hall, student bandmasters were instructed, as part of their studies, to compose a tutor for their particular instruments. When they had all completed their tutors, these were published under Adkins' name. It was also 'suggested' that it might be a good idea if all bandmasters purchased these tutors. It sounds plausible and, if it were true, what an excellent little earner it must have been.

Another comparable problem was waiting for me just around the corner. It was the custom in the regiment to play hockey, and it was decided that the Boys would, if required, be able to admit to at least some basic knowledge of the game. We were given elementary instructions and divided into two teams before being sent forth to do battle. During our first 'friendly' match, I sustained a blow to the mouth, resulting in a loose, soon to be lost, tooth. The knock-on effect of this was that I could now only play an instrument with a larger bore mouth piece than the horn. What else, but the tuba?

From the first moment I played a tuba, a love of the instrument was born that has stayed with me to this very day. I still listen very intently for the bass section – string or brass – in every piece of music I hear.

In my first weeks, Boys were still being enlisted, until eventually we had two huts full of mischievous, cheeky, fun-loving boys, most of whom in a short space of time received a nick-name reflecting some characteristic, physical feature or habit. Many of these names have stuck through the years and are still used whenever we meet.

Cherry [red nose]

Lofty [height]
Conk [big nose]
Sleepy [obvious?]
Bunny [?]
Knecker [long neck]
Buster [civilian nick name]
Ocker [?]
Titch [size]
Deuce [from surname]
Mo [from Christian name]
Spud [from surname]
Doggie[?]
Digger [This nick name came about because on enlistment, when the boy was asked his trade he replied, 'A horticultural worker in a cemetery'. As the recruiting Sergeant couldn't spell horticultural, he entered 'Grave Digger'!

Among the Boys, there were two who had both been pupils at the Hereford Cathedral Choir School and, by coincidence, both had brothers serving with the First Battalion in the Sudan. There was also a Boy whose father had been a Police Superintendent. Another Boy's father was a builder, and another's father was a Council road worker. We came from many different backgrounds but for the most part gelled well together and many have remained friends to this day.

As the days went by and we became not only proficient in playing of our given instruments but also in our knowledge of the elements of music, it was decided we were ready to start playing military marches. The first two chosen were *El Capitan* and *Imperial Echoes*, the latter being the signature tune for the BBC's Sports results programme every Saturday afternoon and a great favourite. Whistled versions of these marches could be heard echoing through the streets of Shrewsbury on many an evening when the Boys were out.

Regular bandsmen were returning to the Depot not only from the unit stationed in Cove, but also from the First Battalion. One could identify which man came from where by beret patches and shoulder titles. The First Battalion wore a square patch of green behind their cap badges while the Second Battalion wore a circular one. The First Battalion wore green titles with gold lettering while the Second Battalion wore white lettering on a red back ground The Depot staff [and Boys] wore a square patch behind the cap badge, but with red titles and white lettering. The permanent staff of the Depot wore a green circular patch, about an inch across, on their upper sleeve. On this patch were the Prince of Wales feathers in red, which was the sign of the Mid West District of Western Command.

As time went on so we became more regimented and somewhat more orderly......

06:30 Reveille. Make up bed. Wash and shave [if required]. Sweep out bed space, also attend to such barrack room duty as detailed.

07:30 Breakfast.

08:30 Muster Parade

09:00 Individual Practice [possible tuition]

10:30 Mid Morning Break.

11:15 Educational training under one of the 'Schoolies'

12:30 Midday meal.

The period between 09:00 and 12:30 could be changed for Drill, Physical Training, Education, while that between 14:00 and 16:30 could be spent on 'Interior Economy' [cleaning of living quarters], kit cleaning, sport or generally trying to keep out of the way until tea at 16:30, after which we were free to take in any legal pastimes available.

Besides our musical training we also, as mentioned, had to attend school for tuition by Sergeants of the Army Education Corps on most General subjects, as taught in ordinary schools, plus Military History, or any other subject the Sergeant happened to be interested at the time. Those deemed bright enough were crammed for their Army Certificate of Education, 1st Class. Obviously it meant Brownie points for the 'schoolie' if a large number sat for this certificate. For myself, I wasn't particularly interested at the time, which was to get me in hot water, when I was paraded in front of the Band President and advised that if my attitude didn't change, I would be considered for discharge as unsuitable for further service.

As the band grew in size and proficiency, we were required to provide music for a 'Dining In' of the Officers Mess. One of the pieces we played, I still recall, was *My Old Stable Jacket*. I also remember that the Boys cleared the Ante Room of every glass of alcohol left there by the Officers when they were called in to dine. From all reports, the waiters were reprimanded for having cleared the Ante Room too quickly.

On another occasion we were required to provide music for the recruits Passing Out parade, of which the inspecting Officer was General Sir Brian Horrocks. General Horrocks was at that time General Officer Commanding Western Command but lately had been Corps Commander of XXXth Corps in Northern Europe. XXXth Corps had had in its number the Fourth Battalion of the KSLI, also the Herefordshire Regiment, both of which were Territorial Battalions of the Regiment. General Horrocks inspected the Band and was clearly impressed when told that a majority of the members were Boys of less than twelve months service.

Boys were still being harried by all and sundry but life had a sweeter side in that when you had attained a reasonable standard you were allowed to 'walk out'.

Boys were allowed out of Barracks on:

Wednesdays   16:30-21:00 hrs.
Saturdays   12:30-22:00 hrs.
Sundays   08:00-21:00 hrs.

Our liberty depended on getting through inspection at the Guard, very often under the gaze of the Provost Sergeant Paddy Ryan, who knowing the Boys were not allowed to 'walk out' in civilian shoes, would ask to see the bottoms of our boots so that he could count the number of studs in the soles (for some unknown reason the requisite number was thirteen). While most of us got through there was one Boy who always seemed to have one or two studs missing.

One evening the Boy in question decided to borrow another Boy's boots. He presented himself for inspection.

Paddy looked at the boots, with their thirteen studs apiece, then at the Boy. 'Who's boots have you got on?' he barked.

However, he let the boy through, I'm sure with a smile on his face.

When we went out there were places we could go without spending too much of our very scarce cash. These were the various Youth Clubs in Shrewsbury, both near and far. The nearest one was held in a church hall in the district of Frankwell (renowned for flooding every year when the River Severn overflows).

This particular club was attended by the rather attractive daughter of a long-service Lance Corporal in the band, who was in the habit of issuing every so often a warning.

'If ever I catch any of you Boys hanging around my daughter – watch out!'

The old adage about pots calling kettles black came to mind, for no matter where the band went to perform, this L/Corporal would produce a little black book, run his finger down the pages and announce that he was going to visit an 'Aunt' during the interval.

The band also played regularly in The Quarry in Shrewsbury and one of the Boys would be detailed to guard the instruments, music and stands during the tea interval. For this responsibility the Boy would receive the princely sum of half-a-crown (12½ p). This may seem a paltry sum today, but as a Boy's pay was 10 shillings (50p) a week, of which he received only half-a-crown, with the remainder kept in credit against any privilege leave he might be granted, this was a princely sum indeed.

After the performance was finished, we would help to pack up the music and stands, load the lorry and take charge of the card cases and buff belts of those not wanting to return to the Barracks. For this we were paid either in coin of the realm, or in cigarettes.

There were still a large number of men returning to the depot who had served both in Egypt and India and it wasn't long before our language was tainted with various words and sayings from both of these distant countries. I still remember a number, some of which have taken root:

Jildi............	Quickly
Char............	Tea
Dhersi..........	Tailor
Rhooti	Bread
Muckin.........	Butter
Shufti............	Look
Cushi............	Easy
Bint	Female
Bondhuck......	Rifle
Charpoy.........	Bed
Pawnee..........	Water
Ghari............	Vehicle

There were many more, which, no doubt, other old soldiers

can recall and I hope they will forgive the omissions.

It was while I was at Shrewsbury that, in a significant moment in British Military, Field Marshal Montgomery became Chief of the Imperial General Staff and set about making the soldier's life a better one.

It was decreed that each soldier would have at least six feet of living space and would be issued with:

Pyjamas, cotton, pairs	2
Underpants, cotton, pairs	2 (to replace Drawers, cotton, long)
Pillow, cotton	1
Sheets, cotton, pairs	1
Locker, bedside, wood	1

The more personal items would be issued against the 1157 of the individual while the other items would be made available through the Company store, to be accounted for on departure. Battle Dress Blouses would be manufactured with the 'open collar' area made in the same material as the outer garment. Up to this point, we'd had to scrub the inner canvas to give a cleaner look. Shirts with collar attached would be made available as soon as possible. Neckties would be issued and would be worn on most occasions, although at this time it did not apply to ceremonial occasions, when the collar of the BD would be fastened.

Another dress change was that the trouser bottoms would be widened to give a smarter look when worn at leisure. (The practice of unofficially widening was paid for by the wearer up until then.) The most significant ruling of CIGS's innovations, which affected everyone, was that no General Officer could carry out the practice of surprise visits, and henceforth must give at least forty eight hours notice of his intention. I know many people gave a sigh of relief at this item.

These innovations were welcomed by most but a few of the old sweats who took the view that the fewer items a soldier had to worry about, the better.

The widening of trouser bottoms did cause some problems in the wearing of 'gaiter weights'. These weights consisted of lead weights threaded onto a leather boot lace or cord at intervals with the ends joined to make it circular, leaving enough inside area to enable you to slip the weight over your boot and up to the knee. Then, when the trousers were pulled up, the weights would fall over the gaiter. In normal use, this was fine, but if an NCO was in a bad mood and demanded that the knees be raised in a faster or higher fashion, the weights could fly up and crack you just below the knee, or the trouser leg might come away from the top of your gaiter, and weights would litter the square.

The Boys were expected to enjoy Physical Training, and I'm afraid the PT Instructors adopted the attitude, 'Enjoy it you will!' Among the instructors at this time were a number of professional footballers, such names as Billy Wright, of Wolverhampton Wanderers and Brown of Stoke, and several others doing their National Service who were not going to allow any snotty nosed Band Boy to get in the way of their departure on a Saturday morning. These men ran us ragged! I particularly disliked the vaulting horse, for which I paid dearly in press-ups.

In recent years, I've watched, with some amusement, a television programme attempting to depict the life of a National Serviceman. The life of a Band Boy was just as hard, especially when under the control of a National Service NCO who didn't want to be in the service and was not going to let anyone or anything get in the way of his future professional life.

A SHROPSHIRE BOY

CHAPTER TWO

Shilling a day, jolly good pay. Lucky to get it, shilling a Day. (Kipling)

As boys always are, we were short of money. My mother used to send me a cake every week, along with a packet of top quality cigarettes. The cake was always a good seller and the cigarettes I would trade in for an inferior brand. While on the subject of cigarettes, a particular incident comes to mind.

As you can imagine men and boys were always running out of cigarettes. 'Save me your douffer,' (which was a fag end) or 'Got a fag I can borrow?' were often heard pleas.

There were, of course, the craftier characters. One corporal used to pull a packet of cigarettes from his pocket, take one out, light it, then, if anyone asked him for one, he would close the packet and cast it to the floor.

'That's my last one,' he would shrug regretfully and leave it where it was until there was no one around to retrieve it and the cigarettes it still contained. Eventually one of the boys cottoned on to what he was doing and asked the usual question.

Receiving the usual answer, he watched the packet descend to the floor, walked over to where the packet lay and crushed

35

it flat with his heel. To say the corporal was not amused would be an understatement.

There followed a long, hard chase around the barrack area which only came to a stop when the band were called for practice.

At one end of the Boy's hut was a section containing the office of the company commander, which brings to mind an incident that still makes me smile. One day a couple of the Boys were playing a form of bayonet practice, using a broom in place of the real thing. All went well until the target boy stepped aside with the result the broom staff was punched through the plaster board partition poking the company commander in the small of the back.

I don't remember the major's exact words but within seconds he and the company sergeant-major appeared in the doorway demanding to know who was the idiot who had caused the major such pain? I feel this was the moment we Boys came together, for not one word was said. For some reason, the broom had been cast to the rafters of the hut and had the offended parties cast their eyes heavenwards, they might have found their culprit.

Another memorable incident also involved the major. A company commander's inspection of living accommodation was due to take place and, as usual, a couple of the boys were fooling about. One threw a boot at the other which missed and sailed through the top pane of a window and landed outside, having smashed the glass en route. The lance-corporal in charge proved to be a quick thinker, and almost before the boot had landed ordered one of the Boys to remove what glass remained in the frame and told me to go outside and remove or bury any glass he could see. These tasks were rapidly carried out, with the dustpan and brush cleaned and replaced for inspection with five minutes to spare before the major and his entourage appeared.

All went well until the major arrived at the window, there he stopped and gazed intently, while we quivered. He removed his swagger cane from beneath his arm, tapped the window frame. 'This is how I want to see all the windows,' he said.

How we stopped ourselves from laughing I do not know, for had he lifted his cane forward another inch, the truth would have been revealed, Needless to say we had to pay for the window pane to be replaced via 'Barrack Damages'. Every so often we would be informed that an amount was being stopped from our pay against 'Barrack Damage', regardless of who had caused any damage. (A nice little earner for somebody?)

As time went by, our musical proficiency improved to a point where some of us could sight read the music put in front of them. Some even progressed to a standard where they could read not only one or two bars ahead (which most trained musicians can do without effort) but as many as four or five. It is interesting that many American artist's prefer to make their recordings in this country as the standard of sight-reading by our musicians is so high that it saves time in rehearsals and recording, thereby saving a lot of money. Indeed, many recording musicians had backgrounds in Boys' service.

During my early days in Shrewsbury, men were coming to the Depot to await demoblisation from the Army, including the Polish Free Corps, who arrived in such numbers that they swamped the hutted area. There were so many of them it was decided that the Band and Boys would be moved to Mount Camp, a hutted camp about a mile from the Barracks and reached via Barrack Lane, which ran behind the rear wall of the married quarters.

The sports field lay along most of the left hand side, with civilian houses on the right. Many of the houses had large gardens containing fruit trees. One contained a large walnut tree which was to prove too much of a temptation for some during their journeys between the barracks and the camp. One lunch time, a bandsman (a former Boy) decided that this walnut tree had evaded his attention long enough and started to throw large sticks at its branches to dislodge the nuts. In a very short space of time he had harvested quite a number, but instead of moving discretely on, he sat down to shell his booty. After a few minutes a gate in the garden wall flew open and a very irate gentleman pounced upon him. The bandsman tried to deny having taken part in the walnut theft, whereupon the house-owner demanded to see the palms of his hands which, of course, were stained a very dark brown with walnut juice. The bandsman was reported but got away with a severe reprimand and a warning, 'Not to be such a bloody fool in the future!'

Mount Camp was under the control of a company sergeant-major, nicknamed Guts and Gaiters, who appeared to have a distinct dislike of the Boys. This was probably because we had our own mess room, rest room, plus a ration scale above the rest of the inhabitants, which involved more paper work for the CSM.

While we were there, the order was given that Boys were not allowed to smoke. Needless to say this created an 'Us & Them' situation and we intended to play this to the full. Half a Nissen hut had been allocated for use as the Boys' rest room, in which had been placed some ancient adjustable arm chairs. These chairs were covered in well-worn leatherette material and we decided the rips and tears would make useful hiding places for cigarettes and other forbidden items. This was soon demonstrated when a number of the boys, including myself, were having a quick drag and the door burst open. There stood Guts and Gaiters, having carried out one of his tiptoe tours of the area. It was obvious we had been smoking as the room was full of tobacco smoke.

'Who was it?' he asked.

No one replied. When the door had burst open I had dropped a packet containing five cigarettes down between the padded cushion and the frame of my chair, or so I thought. Guts and Gaiters cast his eye about the room and saw the packet sticking out from under the chair. When the inevitable question was asked, I admitted the packet belonged to me and was instructed to wait outside until he had finished.

I wondered what was coming next but I never imagined what he had in mind. On joining me outside the CSM beckoned me to follow him, which I did, until we arrived at the coke store [fuel, not a fizzy drink]. This was an open-ended construction, c15' x 15' divided down the middle by a partition of railway sleepers almost eight feet high. Leaning against the wall was a shovel, GS, which the CSM instructed me to grasp in my sweaty hands and throw all the coke on my side over the partition to the other side (and I had a distinct feeling he had planned this before he came into the rest room).

I set to with a will but soon realised that moving coke with a shovel, GS, instead of a coke fork was going to take a long, long time as more fell off the shovel blade than went over the partition. For those not familiar with the Shovel, GS, the shaft was about a yard long, the blade about a foot in length from where the shaft married into the blade to the point at the tip, and the blade some ten inches across its widest point with a crease down the middle. Many men have been grateful for this shovel and its digging potential when under fire but at this point I had a distinct dislike of it.

I laboured on until it was too dark, never knowing when the CSM might reappear, as he did from time to time. I returned as instructed the next evening. Eventually I completed my task and reported to the CSM that I had completed the work. He grimly inspected my efforts with a short bark.

'Now throw it all back!'

People today might consider this bullying but at the time it was accepted as part of a soldier's life.

You got caught – you paid the price!

Near the camp, the River Severn passed through a steep-sided and heavily wooded gorge on its way to Shrewsbury and the boys used to spend some of their free time hanging about in this area, despite notices nailed to some of the trees advocating, 'Beware, Adders'.

Whether or not there were any adders we never discovered and I still wonder today if the notices were placed there simply to deter ramblers and Boy soldiers.

One evening a group of us were lounging about there when we observed a figure working his way upstream in a coracle. Coracles are a notoriously unstable craft at the best of times and the occupant was having a difficult time maintaining an even passage. We suddenly realised that the oarsman was none other than the company sergeant-major of Head Quarter Company. Being Boys, we decided to help him on his way by dropping large stones in the vicinity of the coracle. How the

CSM kept the craft afloat I do not know and with the wisdom of age now realise that what we did was not only downright stupid but also very dangerous. Whether or not the CSM ever found out who had bombarded him, we never knew but I do know that on our return to HQ Company proper, there seemed an awfully large number of small irritating jobs that needed our attention.

Anyone of my age will recall that the winter of 1946/7 was particularly severe and it was rumoured that the Boys might be sent to their homes as the Army could not take the responsibility for their welfare under such conditions. Each hut received a coke ration every two days. This was hopelessly inadequate in those conditions and was always used up well before the next issue, so the Boys set about adding to this meagre allowance.

In the centre of the camp was a stack of mine crates, beside a sign, 'These crates are not to be removed.' We discovered that if you carefully removed crates from the inner part if the stack, it looked much the same as before. Over a short space of time the heap (or what was left of it) was removed to supplement the Barracks ration. We naturally gave a helping hand and managed to divert some for our own use.

In another bid for supplementary fuel, one of the boys who lived in Shrewsbury got hold of a Gurkha Kukri from somewhere and decided to help things along by chopping branches from the trees. One of the trees overhung a frozen pond, which the boy had to climb, making his way out onto a branch and starting to chop – yes, you've guessed – between himself and the trunk! Result? Down came branch, Boy and Kukri into the freezing water, much to the amusement of those gathered to watch. To give the boy credit, he did retrieve the Kukri and branch, which he dragged to our hut for others to break up.

We did survive that winter, with the help of various means including the use of our great coats as an extra blanket, plus wearing every piece of spare underclothes, both day and night. This may not have been too hygienic but we are still here and we kept the stove going!

It had been suggested that the Boys should form a football team with the idea that they would make their presence noticed in the locality and encourage future recruits. As can be expected the question of a 'strip' arose, and it was decided that the boys would raise a third of the cost of them, with the other two thirds being provided by the Band and Regimental amenities fund, on condition that the strip would be available to any sports team the Boys might form. A meeting held to determine the colour and make up of the shirts decided that they would be gold with a black pocket on which a gold Band harp was embroidered. The badge was the same pattern as worn on the sleeve of Bandsmen. The shorts would be black but until funds were available to purchase these, the team would wear shorts as issued. Football boots would be drawn from the sports store as required. We pleased at least one of the PT instructors, for the colour we had chosen was the same as Wolverhampton Wanderers, the team he played for. Not that it made any difference in his attitude toward us. Amazingly, the strip was still in use when the present day Light Infantry was formed in 1962.

I'm sure many of the ex-Boys would agree that we looked very smart and efficient in our new kit. Our footballing abilities, however, left a lot to be desired. If my memory serves me correctly, in the first season we lost all but one of our matches by scores too horrendous to specify. In our number there were one or two boys with some real skill, but their efforts must have been hampered by the rest of us, who all seemed to have two left feet when it really mattered. The best part of the season was the evening of the League's Annual General Meeting and presentation of prizes, which was held in the saloon bar of *The Slipper*, a pub in the town. No one ever queried our ages as we were wearing the King's uniform, with the result we returned to barracks a little worse for wear.

I should mention here the Salop Mafia. Over the years, many ex-members of the KSLI have settled in Shrewsbury and you could bet a pound to a penny that the Guard Room telephone would ring and someone would be waiting for the offender be he regular soldier, National Serviceman or Boy upon his arrival at the gates.

In the late 1940s, television was not available to most of the populace and, in general, entertainment as well as education was found through talks, lectures and cinemas. For us Boys anything that didn't cost money was more than welcome. One such event was a series of talks under the heading *Musical Appreciation* given in the Headquarters of Mid West district in the Coleham area of the town. It was usually on one of the nights when Boys should be in barracks but release from barracks was not the only reason we made every effort to attend. There were a large number of ATS girls stationed and working in the Headquarters and many attended the talks, if only for the tea and biscuits, while we attended primarily to chat up these young ladies.

Our restricted hours of liberty did not allow a great deal of time for courting but one or two relationships did stand the strain of the 2100 hours curfew. In fact one such relationship blossomed into marriage which, I was recently informed, is still going strong.

One of the boys decided to use his limited musicianship in his courting tactics. One evening he took his alto saxophone out of barracks (against the rules) and proceeded to serenade the girl on the grass bank above the river by playing *Met a Gal in Calico*, over and over again.

I only discovered this when another boy and I were making our way via the Quarry back to barracks. We'd heard the wailing tones of the saxophone and decided to investigate.

The ideas previously put forward by Field Marshal Montgomery began to take effect. One of these drew the Boys not only into the system but also provided some of us with a nice little earner. It appeared that National Service recruits were to be given every assistance during their first hours/days in the service. As the recruit entered the Keep, he would be allocated a Boy to take him through his kit issue. There was to be no more, 'Hold your kit bag open while I chuck in your items.'

Every item was checked not only by the recruit but also by the Boy before the recruit signed for it on his 1157 (much to the annoyance of the storemen). The recruit would also be given the opportunity to check the comfort of his ammunition boots. He would walk the length of the stores carrying in each hand a sand filled ammunition box. Having tested both pairs of boots he was then taken to rejoin the intake but before we departed he would be asked his hut number and given a not too gentle hint that for a small remuneration we would call round later and give a hand with blancoing and polishing.

The boys involved would get themselves into gangs of four. Having found a receptacle to hold the blanco liquid, the first Boy would coat the piece of equipment in the liquid then hang it on the barbed wire strung between the posts that lined the walkways between the huts. The second Boy got to work with a Brasso rag and applied polish to all the brass work. The third Boy polished off the Brasso then passed the item to the fourth boy who reassembled the equipment. When we all agreed we had done a fair job we returned the items to their owners and collected our dues. As this was going against the Boy/man ruling we had to be fairly careful. But there's no doubt some of the boys walked out of an evening with more money in their pockets than a lot of the men.

Boys were still being enlisted but at nowhere near the former rate, which brings to mind an incident that showed just how cruel young people can be unknowingly. One Boy who had enlisted, soon became very listless and spent a lot of time draped over a radiator near his bed space. We naturally failed too realise that something was seriously amiss. Instead of reporting the Boy's condition we did little else but poke fun and taunt him. Eventually, when he failed to parade for morning muster, he was ordered to report sick and was diagnosed as suffering with diabetes. He was discharged from the service and the last I heard, he had been granted a medical pension. It's fair to point out, though, that at the time there was no NCO living in the huts occupied by the Boys. Had there been, there's no doubt the sick Boy's condition would have been brought much sooner to the attention of our seniors.

As I mentioned earlier, Military bands of those days carried out engagements on behalf of councils and boroughs all over the country and it was while returning from one such engagement that our band became involved in an accident with a three ton lorry. On the day in question the lorry carrying the band was travelling down a steep hill when the driver realised he had no effective brakes. He did, however, notice that there was a lay-by on the bend at the bottom of the hill. As he had little option, he steered into the lay-by only realising at the last second that there was a family sitting beside their car having a picnic. (Why people sit in lay-bys having picnics, I still don't understand.)

To avoid hitting them all, he managed to steer into a bank at the back of the lay-by, which caused the three-tonner to tip on its side and slide along for some distance. The bandsmen riding in the rear along with the boxes, stands and instruments hadn't realised what was happening and thus were fairly relaxed, otherwise there might have been some serious injuries. Luckily the family picnicking were shocked but unhurt, and after helping everyone from the capsized vehicle, provided us with tea and comfort. The father of the family took the bandmaster in his car to find a telephone to arrange transport for the bandsmen back to Shrewsbury. This was to be the first of a number of accidents involving the band and three ton lorries, and I got the distinct feeling that the band of the KSLI and three ton lorries were not completely compatible.

How nice of you to drop by. One lump or two?

Soon after this, for reasons beyond my comprehension, I was sent to Norton Barracks, Worcester for training. I could only assume that I might have been deemed likely to develop a better attitude away from my own Depot, as I would have received exactly the same training under the guidance of the Depot staff.

A SHROPSHIRE BOY

I was placed in a platoon of National Service conscripts, all of whom did not want to be there, and it seemed that whinging and complaining were the order of the day.

It also appeared that the instructions relating to Boys and men not mixing had gone by the board, although the Worcester Boys had their own accommodation. I suppose I was fortunate in that I had some experience of drill and equipment and thus was able to give the conscripts a helping hand when they got lost in a maze of webbing. I was issued a full set of webbing plus rifle, and as I knew my way around was able to take things a little easier than the rest of the platoon. The SMLE rifle had woodwork of the most beautiful deep red and I discovered that a quick wipe over with the cloth used to polish the barrack room floor brought a beautiful sheen to the wood, although I had to keep a tight grip when carrying out drill with the rifle.

However, all was not sweetness and light, as I found out on our first visit to the rifle ranges. The rifle had a kick like a mule and you had to keep it very, very tight into your shoulder.

One matter that did cause a lot of verbal resentment was the fact that Boys were excused some wearisome duties like cook house fatigues. At this time the Army wasn't flush with money and although a large number of the recruits thought cook house fatigues were a punishment, it was an essential task, for although potatoes were passed through a peeling machine they still had to have the eyes removed by hand, and men had to be detailed for the task. The corporal in charge of the platoon explained that because of the Boys' status and low pay, which he felt burden enough, they were excused fatigues, but the grumbling carried on until the corporal suggested I could volunteer, at the same time casting a knowing look in my direction. It did not take me long to agree as I knew that he also made out the rosters for the fatigue duties. I found myself walking along behind a horse-drawn, two-wheeled cart around the barracks, picking up any pieces of waste that happened to fall during the emptying of various bins outside the offices and barrack blocks. Very cushy, unless the horse deposited manure on the road.

To deal with this I was issued with a dust pan and brush and ordered to place my collection in a special bin at the rear of the cart. I was informed that the contents would be used on the rose bushes outside the Officers' Mess.

As with all intensive training, we were harried at every turn but I was surprised just how quickly the conscripts adapted and became presentable and fairly good soldiers, and could therefore be let loose on the good inhabitants of Worcester.

In Worcester at this time the Corn Exchange was being used as a canteen and rest place for the large number of troops stationed not only in the immediate area but also training in the Malvern Hills. There was a large number of Engineer Regiments training there, including many volunteers from the Netherlands and Belgium who were to provide the nucleus of the rebuilt armies of their countries.

To say the Corn Exchange was bulging would be no exaggeration. The highlight of the evening was not finding an empty chair but somewhere to place it! We managed, but not all our time was spent drinking tea, for in a nearby narrow side street was the house of an elderly lady who brewed her own beer which she served in Royal Worcester china pint mugs which, no doubt, she paid for with free pints. I tried the brew and must admit that it was distinctly more-ish, although two pints was usually enough for me.

During our training at Worcester we were given talks by the Platoon Officer on subjects chosen by the Army Bureau of Current Affairs, intended to prepare men for a return to civilian life. I could not see any rhyme or reason for these as we were in a unit full of National Service conscripts who had only just left civilian life and were hardly likely to have forgotten what the outside world held for them. In addition, those soldiers in the unit had a long time to serve and weren't really interested.

I also encountered several other inexplicable military practices. One of these concerned steel helmets. After they had been issued to us we had to hand them back into stores so they could be painted. While the paint was still wet they had sand sprayed on them. On receiving our helmets back again we applied a coat of the blanco (which was khaki, by the way, not white), in use at the time on our equipment. Fine so far, but then we had to scrape and polish the rim It seemed to me a very strange practice, to dull the helmet then shine the rim – a complete contradiction of purposes.

Half way through our training it was announced that one of the older, retired officers would be inspecting the company. We formed up on the square and there approached a figure that I am sure the late Peter Sellers used as the basis for one of his characters. The officer approached – or should I say creaked – across the square, and was greeted with the customary salute before proceeding to inspect the parade.

On reaching me he gazed intently at my cap badge then asked how long I had been in the service. When I answered him he seemed quite baffled and turned to the parade commander. 'I felt sure,' he said, 'that I was to inspect the passing out parade of senior men.'

We were also introduced to the Gas Bunker. Before entering the bunker we had to adjust our gas-masks to ensure a close fit. We then entered the bunker and as we did so the door was closed behind us and the NCO already inside placed a small pellet upon the top of the lighted stove in the centre of the floor. After some minutes we were told to remove our masks and make our way out of the bunker with the added instruction, 'Do not rub your eyes.'

Those nearest the door thought they were going to get away lightly but the NCO had other ideas and placed himself in the doorway and made them go round again. As can be expected our eyes streamed with tears and again we were instructed not to rub our eyes but to let the fresh air clear them. I wonder how many servicemen went through this uncomfortable procedure. The next time I wore a gas mask was during rehearsal of procedures in case the Russians crossed the border into West Germany.

The remainder of our training seemed to go fairly well. We 'passed out' and were granted seven days' privilege leave, after which I was posted back to the Depot to rejoin the band. I must admit I enjoyed this period of my service despite the intensive aspects, such as forced marches and pressure intended to make a soldier think for himself. At least I could look the duty soldier in the eye, having had an insight into how the other half lived.

All through my service, duty men always voiced the opinion that the band led a cushy life, to which we always replied, 'When you're working, we are practising, and when you are at leisure, we're working!'

One major event in my life at this time was the first sprouting of my beard. One morning the platoon corporal gazed at me and asked when I had last shaved. I replied that I did not shave.

'You do now!' he said, and I was sent to the barrack room to collect my towel, razor (complete with blade) and shaving soap. The lance corporal was told to escort me to the ablutions and there started the daily habit that has been with me ever since.

On my return to the band in Shrewsbury, I renewed a friendship with one of the boys from Hereford and on many occasions spent week-ends at his home, an hour's train journey away. I often think the warm-hearted kindness shown to me by his parents as amongst the dearest memories I have.

Boys travelled at this time at a cheaper rate on the railways using what was called Boy Soldiers' rate – about half the normal. In exchange for the requested fare you received a ticket – actually half a ticket, as it had been cut diagonally across. Rail tickets at this time were oblong cards with a perforation across the centre and the name of the destination printed horizontally across the face. With the ticket being cut in such a fashion I often wondered how the ticket collectors read the destination, although I never heard of anyone having any trouble.

One day we were told to move into another hut. I never discovered why. On entering our new home I found that the wooden pegs were missing from the wall board so I returned to my old dwelling to remove the pegs I had left behind. I was quite happily doing this when one of the new occupants, a Boy, entered the hut and asked me what I thought I was doing. 'That's fairly obvious,' I said.

I was told to leave the pegs alone.

'B———s!' I replied.

To say the other boy was bigger than me would be no understatement. (He wore a size 12 boots at the age of sixteen.) He was about to belt me when the l/corporal in charge of Boys arrived. He obviously heard or had been told what was happening. He informed us that we would meet in the Gymnasium – 'with the gloves on' – at 16:30. I stood at this time about 5'6" and weighed about 8st while my adversary stood at least 6' in his socks and weighed in at over 11st.

At 16:30 the gloves went on and battle commenced. I did fairly well until my opponent landed one almighty blow on my nose which caused me to see a galaxy of stars and gave me a bloody nose. At this point the l/corporal felt honour had been served and stepped in to stop the bout, while the other Boy and I became friends and remained so throughout our service.

Around about this time, War Gratuities were paid and for some reason I received £5, which I placed into a Post Office savings account to which I added whenever memory or circumstances allowed. I still remember the account number although I feel it would not be prudent to give it here. One thing resulting from these payments, which sticks in my mind was that a lot of card schools sprang up and I witnessed one man losing all his gratuity on one turn of a card, playing Shoot. The man was so shaken by the experience, he went straight to the Orderly Room and signed on for further service.

Two other significant events took place about this time. The first was the arrival of a new Band Sergeant who had done duty in various parts of the then Empire so he brought not only worldly knowledge but also musical knowledge, both of which he deployed to keep us from the direct attention of the authorities.

The other event concerned me personally. One day the BM told me to tidy myself up a bit as I was going to see the Band President (he with the hearing aid). We entered the office of the BP who, after adjusting his hearing aid, informed me I was to be promoted to Boy, lance corporal, for which I would receive one penny a day or two shillings and sixpence a month from the Band fund (12½p in today's coinage). I was so amazed I could hardly answer. *Why me?* I thought.

On leaving the office, the bandmaster told me to go back to my billet, collect my battle dress and overcoat, and take them to the tailors' shop and inform them of my requirements. The tailor was known for being a bit of a leg-puller. He gave me a hard time but eventually sewed the stripes on my BD blouse with a gentle hint that when I was old enough I could buy him a pint in the *Bricklayers*, this being the pub nearest to the Depot.

As with most army tales there was a sting in the tail. As I was walking back to my billet I was confronted by a particularly nasty corporal in the Band who demanded to know whose blouse I was wearing. I tried to explain but, being the pig-headed person he was, he wouldn't listen. He informed me he was placing me under close arrest and would be charging me with impersonating an NCO. Off we marched to the guard room where he placed me in the charge of the Regimental Police.

I must admit I felt fairly relaxed over the whole happening as I knew I was in the right. Strange how good it feels when you know everything is on your side. On his return from lunch the Provost Sergeant entered the guard room and demanded to know what I was doing in his guardroom. He was given the facts, not only by me, but also the Regimental Police.

'Leave it to me,' he said with quiet menace.

He rang the company office and told whoever answered the phone that he wanted Corporal X at the guardroom now, if not sooner! The sergeant then rang the WO & Sergeants' Mess and had a conversation with the bandmaster. The corporal arrived at the guardroom and was asked by the sergeant to accompany him into one of the cells. We were able to hear only snatches of the conversation.

'Next time, get your facts straight before placing anyone in my guardroom, otherwise you might be next!'

The corporal left looking very disgruntled and gave me one hell of a look.

Having taken on the job, I also took the flak. The first time I took the Boys to the cookhouse for their meal and told the men to stand back to let the Boys through, I was addressed in terms that made me wonder about my parentage. One recruit was giving full verbal flow until his mate told him to be careful.

'He's only a frigging boy!' the recruit replied.

'Yes, but he's got the stripe!'

I felt about ten feet tall.

What did take getting used to was still living in the same hut as the Boys with whom I had been since enlistment. There were, of course, one or two boys who tried it on, but without getting too heavy I think I coped. I held the rank for nearly a year but cannot recall any other Boy being promoted.

When eventually the Band and Boys moved back to the barracks proper, the Boys, predictably, got up to all sorts of pranks. Above the ablutions was a room designated as a drying room. During cold spells the Boys took over this room as a practice area which, in turn, led to a brush with the law. The drying room was reached by an outside stairway consisting of wooden steps c 3' feet wide, rising to a platform roughly 8' from the ground. The platform was about a yard square and gave a view over the rear gardens of the houses some fifty yards away.

One snowy day one of the boys spotted two police officers (complete with helmets) approaching the back door of one of the houses. As they moved between the house and an outbuilding, the Boy loosed a snowball and we knew from the shout that went up that he'd scored a hit. When the two policemen came back into view, we saw that the snowball had struck the side of one of their helmets. Needless to say we disappeared rather quickly. The next thing we knew we were told to parade in the walkway between the huts and reveal the name of the boy who had thrown the snowball. The Boys once again showed their solidarity and said nothing We were warned about our future behaviour and that appeared to be the end of that particular incident but I am sure a wary eye was kept on us for some time.

Boys were not the only ones to indulge in a bit of leg-pulling. Bandsmen who had been Boys in the past certainly played jokes on the Boys, especially those newly enlisted.

Many a Boy was asked, 'Where's the "long weight" needed to clean this clarinet/oboe/saxophone?'

On admitting that he didn't know, the Boy would be dispatched to the Band stores to ask for a long wait for his instrument. The storemen, of course, were ready to oblige.

Other favourites were: 'Where's the elbow grease for this trombone slide?' or 'Where's the turn key for the valves on this cornet/ tuba/euphonium?'

The storeman's reply usually went some thing like, 'Sorry, I'm right out but I've got some on order. Come back in a couple of days.'

Many did come back, especially if the joke was carried on by those in the same billet. Luckily the bandmaster and most of the NCOs took a light-hearted attitude after asking the Boy why he was hanging around the band stores.

CHAPTER THREE

Here will I smell my remnant out, and tie my life within this band. (Herbert)

I came on to service on reaching the age of 17½. This event showed, once again, how a young soldier had been conned, for although you transferred your belongings into a man's hut, your actual colour service did not start until you reached the age of eighteen, thus the Army got six months of your life for nothing!

Around this time a number of us were allowed to 'turn in' with the Band proper and so became eligible to be selected for the concert band, with the opportunity to be paid for our efforts. I still recall the thrill and pride I felt on reading my name on the list of bandsmen chosen for a performance in public. At last I was going to show that all the months of practice and tuition had not been a waste of time. I was also to learn that the bandstand on a concert day attracted girls like a honey pot attracts bees and I'll always remember my first paid engagement.

It was an afternoon and evening engagement in Canon Hill Park, Birmingham. Here I first saw the notorious Black Book belonging to the L/Corporal who warned off the band boys from his daughter. With hindsight, maybe his own activities were the reason for the warnings.

After the thrill of reading your name on the Band list for an engagement, you started to pray that you didn't play any wrong notes or drop a wind iron.

A wind iron was a piece of heavy metal bar about 12" long and 1½" wide with a hooked part at one end to be placed over the sheet music, music pad and stand to stop any wind from blowing the music away. Usually there would be one placed right, left and centre which from time to time had to be moved to allow a page of music to be turned over. If you think that's easy, try it with one hand while holding your instrument in the other. Heaven help you if you dropped one, even in the gap between musical items. It could cost you dear!

If the bandmaster was in a foul mood he might fine you five shillings, to be deducted from your engagement money. I survived my first outing without dropping a note or a wind iron, and felt proud of myself.

Shortly after this the Band was posted to join the 2nd Battalion, which was stationed at Bicester in Oxfordshire. The men of the battalion were engaged in mothballing 25-pounder field guns in the Command Ordnance Depot. Our accommodation consisted of large Nissen huts and, I believe, had started life as a camp for American troops prior to D-Day. The huts contained the most efficient pot-bellied stoves I've ever come across – much more efficient than their British counterparts With the relatively small coke ration we received they gave the most wonderful warmth right through the hut. No more huddling round the stove with your overcoat on.

At Bicester I learned a drill movement I hadn't come across before, nor since. Every morning the battalion would muster on the edge of the square but in no particular order. When the Regimental Sergeant Major arrived, the order would be given: 'Get on the move!'

The battalion would come to attention, turn to their right and march across to a point where the Senior WO or Sergeant present would give the order to turn about. This would go on until the Platoon or Company markers were set. (The reader might be interested to note that the Light Infantry commence most of their movements from the 'At ease' position.) The next order would be: 'Join your markers!'

How we managed to carry out this command is still a matter of wonderment to me as we had to cut across others trying to do the same thing. But we survived.

Within recent, uncomfortable memory of war, the nation was still full of wartime fervour and patriotic regard for its forces. Parades such as *Salute the Soldier* and *Wings Week* were regularly being held. So it came about that the Band and Bugles were invited to provide the music for such a parade in Oxford.

We set off at a steady, Heavy Infantry pace (about 118 paces to the minute) and all went well until one of the Buglers got the heel plate of his boot trapped between the tar blocks of the roadway. He stopped dead! The Buglers behind him side stepped and missed him but the first Bandsman (a tuba player) hit him square in the back. The Band as far back as the cymbal player piled up like a concertina. The cymbal player, though, saw in time what was happening and was able to lead those behind him around the problem. Everything got sorted out before the passing of the troops marching behind, but it was a near thing.

A moment of bluff is worth the telling. I still smile at the memory of it. Every evening at 18:00 hours, 'Retreat' is sounded and the Regimental flag lowered by one of the Regimental Police. On duty with the Bugler was a trainee who throughout the day had performed well, but when it came to 'Retreat', he wasn't feeling so confident. The Bugler told him to take his position between the flag pole and the Orderly Officer and go through the motions. The Bugler himself would play.

Picture if you will the guard room with one window open slightly at the bottom, a Regimental Policeman about ten yards in front preparing to lower the flag with, two yards to the right of the flagpole, the trainee bugler, with the Orderly Officer three yards away with the defaulters. The trainee raised he bugle to his lips, as instructed, and went through the motions while the Bugler sounded through the gap in the window and no one was the wiser, in fact the Provost Sergeant congratulated the trainee on a wonderful sound.

Head Quarter Company at this time was commanded by a major who had been in the Glider Pilot Regiment and believed in being fair with the men under his command.

One weekend a bandsman waiting for a train on Bicester

station was approached by two Military Policemen who demanded to see what he had in the attaché case he was carrying. When the case was opened it revealed several bars of soap (which at this time was fairly scarce). The MPs arrested him and took him back to the camp where they placed him in the charge of the Regimental Police, who directly the MPs had gone released the man into the camp on his word, saying they were sorry but they couldn't let him go home.

On Monday the MPs returned and the man was taken before the Company Commander. After hearing the evidence the major asked the MPs one question: 'Can you prove the soap in this man's possession was stolen?'

Of course, they could not and the case was dismissed, but before sending the MPs on their way the major had a last word. 'If any man in my company wants to save his soap ration to take home to his family I will not stop him. I suggest you stop looking for easy pinches.'

The bandsman was dismissed and breathed a sigh of relief. (The major himself was later killed in Korea, which gives thought to the saying, *'The good die young'*.)

Most weekends were free. In fact, I caught a bus to Bedford from Bicester Market Place nearly every week and could spend days at home. It certainly made a change from staying in camp.

After a few weeks the Band was on the move again, this time to Bury, where they took up residence in Wellington Barracks, the Depot of the Lancashire Fusiliers, while the 2nd Battalion went to Oswestry.

You may have gathered that the Bands of the two battalions

had been very quietly merged together into one Regimental Band and although we didn't realise it at the time, it was the beginning of the reduction of Regiments of the British Army.

Bury being fairly convenient for Manchester, we had the opportunity to sample the city's night life. It was during such a visit that I got into conversation with a member of one of the Scottish regiments who offered me some advice: 'The only way in life is to defend yourself against the rest.'

He then proceeded to show me how he had a razor blade sewn into the back rim of his Tam-o-Shanter, which he assured me he had used. We continued chatting for some time until he said he had to go to the toilet, then left the table In what seemed like seconds, two MPs appeared in the bar, asked to see my pay book and wanted to know what I was doing in Manchester. From what they were saying I gained the impression that some one had tipped them off about the presence of the Scotsman, and also that he was a known trouble-maker. Lesson learned: 'Always be guarded with strangers.'

In the barracks there was a stable in which lived a pony – the regimental mascot of the Lancashire Fusiliers – which was cared for and tended by a L/Corporal who held the title of 'Pony Major'. This NCO was rather particular who he let hold the bridle for the taking of photographs. However one of the Band Boys persuaded the Pony Major to let him hold the pony's reins for a photograph. At the crucial moment the pony lashed out with its hind legs. The boy released the bridle and the pony took off across the square, through the gate and down the road to the town. Luckily the traffic was nowhere near as dense as it would be today and the pony was eventually stopped by a police officer who, being an ex-Fusilier, recognised it and awaited the arrival of the Pony Major and the pursuing crowd. What a sight that was – about thirty persons, soldiers, civilians, male and female, all in full cry after the poor animal.

One day the bandmaster informed us that we were to proceed to Liverpool to 'play in' the troopship bringing home the 1st Battalion from Khartoum. (It had been rumoured at one time that the band might join the battalion in the Sudan. From what I learned later, I am glad we didn't.)

As the troopship was docking in the fairly early hours we spent the previous night in a transit camp situated in Bluebell Lane, on the outskirts of the city. To say the camp was grotty – to use a Liverpudlian term – would be an understatement! The whole area was filthy while the huts looked as though they hadn't been cleaned for years, and the bedding issued was indescribable. One can only assume that the state of the camp came about because those passing through spent one night there, at the most, while going to or from the troop dock. We felt, though, that at least the blankets could have been laundered once in a while.

The first thing we did was to ask that the blankets be changed. The storeman naturally refused, causing a fierce argument and some of the blankets were thrown back over the counter. The situation could have got out of hand but for the arrival of the camp sergeant-major who threatened that if we didn't disperse we would be placed under close arrest. (I have often wondered how the camp permanent staff would have faired if charges had been brought against us. Maybe we could have done a good turn for any future transients, but we shall never know.)

I and one or two others decided to find a bed elsewhere and set off through the streets of Liverpool. On our way we met two local coppers, whom we informed of our quest.

'You don't want to go down there,' they said. 'Come with us and we'll point you in the direction of the YMCA.'

The two officers did better than point us in the right direction, they took us to the hostel where they were assured that there were beds available. Before they left we asked why they had stopped us from going down that particular street. They replied that it was one of the worst in the city and they doubted that we would have lasted very long....

After a good night's sleep, an early call plus a cup of tea, we walked in through the camp gates (open), past the guard room and its occupants (fast asleep) in time to secure bread, butter, jam and a cup of tea (at least the water had been boiled). I refrained from taking the porridge on offer as I would have hated to guess what it had been stirred with.

We were transported to the Albert Dock, arriving just as the troopship was docking, and as we marched on we were greeted with all manner of comments and ribald remarks from those on the open deck or gazing from port holes. Little did we realise what part the Albert Dock was to play in our lives in the not too distant future. The band completed its part in the proceedings so returned to Bury to collect our belongings before joining the 1st Battalion in Hermitage Camp, Wrexham.

Boarding the train that was to transport us to our future residence, we were greeted by one of the local girls who had been going out with one of the band. The girl was carrying a parcel which, just before our departure she placed in the bandsman's hands. When all the farewells had been said the lad opened the parcel to discover it contained pigs' trotters. Now pigs' trotters are notoriously greasy at the best of times but in the close confines of a railway carriage they are lethal! It wasn't long before most of the occupants were sporting at least one grease spot. The chap in question wasn't popular for many days, and was given some harsh advice about his future love life.

Hermitage Camp was a hutted establishment situated behind the Depot of the Royal Welch Fusiliers (which is the correct spelling). When everyone had settled in there commenced a series of parades, held in preparation for the Amalgamation, although we were to learn they were also for another, equally momentous occasion.

The amalgamation of the two battalions took place on the square of the Depot in Shrewsbury. The parade took the usual form for such an occasions: Two representative bodies formed upon the square in three ranks, with both battalion colours in the centre, facing a dais upon which stood the Colonel of the Regiment, General Grover CB, MC who after inspecting the two guards gave the order: 'The 1st and 2nd Battalions of the King's Shropshire Light Infantry will amalgamate.'

'Right and Left turn.'

A SHROPSHIRE BOY

'Slow March.'

When the two bodies had fused together they turned to face the front and the order was given. 'With colours flying, the King's Shropshire Light Infantry will advance in review order.'

I can assure you there was scarcely a dry eye on that occasion.

On our return to camp I was instructed to move my bedding and kit into the Band stores and take on the role of assistant to the L/Corporal already in situ. The main duties of a band storeman are to maintain the instruments, issue any music the bandmaster may require for concert work and to keep a record of every item in his charge so that it is known who has got what at any time. Being in the stores gave me the opportunity to try and make the grade on a second instrument. I rather liked the possibilities that the baritone saxophone offered, although I have to admit that I did not make the grade, so back in to its case it went to await the next keen bandsman.

The band were requested to provide the music for the Passing Out parade of the Senior Company of Officer Cadets being trained at the Officer Cadet Training Unit at Eaton Hall, near Chester. Eaton Hall is the country seat of the Dukes of Westminster and was a grand and impressive building. Of course many of the artefacts had been removed but nonetheless it had that something about it that leaves a lasting impression. Sadly it has since been demolished and replaced with something resembling a block of hard cheese.

We marched rapidly on to the parade field in our usual Light Infantry style, which caused the RSM (Coldstream Guards) almost to burst a blood vessel. I well remember his comment. 'I don't want any of that fancy foot work around here!'

I believe the bandmaster and the RSM got into serious talk in the WO and Sgts' Mess, with the result that we marched on at their pace, then, when the parade was over and a fair off, away we marched past the saluting base at our own Light Infantry pace.

The Sword of Honour Cadet was from the Royal Engineers, so we played the parade off with the RE regimental march *Wings*.

Another request for our services was to attend the Open Day of a Heavy Anti-Aircraft Training Regiment, stationed near Tywyn on the North Wales coast. The camp was reached through narrow lanes with very little passing room for three ton lorries. As we proceeded aboard our TCV (Troop Carrying Vehicle) another TCV loaded with ATS girls came from the opposite direction. As there was no convenient passing place the two drivers decided to take a chance. So, warning everybody to keep their elbows well away from the vehicle sides, they began their attempt.

The inevitable happened. The two lorries collided and damage was done. Some time was spent fabricating stories for the filling out of accident report forms. We eventually got under way again and reached the camp none the worse for wear, although the bandmaster wasn't too pleased.

The Band had been allocated a spot some fifty yards to the rear of the guns which were emplaced on the cliff edge over looking the sea. There was a large number of civilians in attendance to see their boyfriends/sons/ brothers pass out from their training. All went well until the part in the programme where the recruits were required to show off their skills at gun drill and firing their weapons.

There was a stiff breeze blowing off the sea towards the area where we were seated, so when the guns were fired, all the sulphur waste and explosive detritus from the gun muzzles showered back on us. We didn't take a great deal of notice at the time but when we came to use our instruments again we discovered that all the brass instruments had been pitted by the waste. The gunners were not our best friends that day.

The powers, recognising that a large number of skilful and expensively trained musicians had been killed in the War, decided that the Bandsmen would henceforward be non-combatant. However we could still be called on as stretcher bearers (bullets can tell?). Away went all our webbing but the Army being what it is, one got away with nothing. It was decided our pay would be linked to our proficiency as musicians.

As we went about our duties, the rifle companies were being drilled and re-kitted, which caused many rumours to fly round the battalion, especially when drafts from other Light Infantry regiments in the Brigade arrived. One incident which took place concerned a draft from the Durham Light Infantry, who refused to re-badge, and created such a rumpus that they were posted out again rather rapidly. We thought this a weak move but with the passing of time it was realised it was better not to have them in our midst.

One evening it appeared on company orders that the Band and Bugles would parade the next day wearing their best battle dress and best boots. At this time my best was of Canadian design and as my Second best was fairly new, I decided to take a chance. The fact was my best BD was not only of Canadian design and manufacture, but also a different colour, style and material. The colour was greener than our drab khaki; the material was smoother and the collar designed with collar and tie in mind, and anyway I LIKED IT!

The inspection was made by the CO, the Adjutant, and the RSM. The CO took some time looking at me and I'm sure he knew what I was up to but in the end said the magic word, 'No exchange,' and moved on.

I breathed a sigh of relief as I realised I was to keep my best Battle Dress, and would be able to use my 2nd B/D for whatever may come.

Everybody was wondering what was going on. We found out one day when the Band and Bugles were put through their paces on the square. There appeared on the edge of the square a Warrant Officer of the Welsh Guards accompanied by two of our Pioneers who were carrying buckets and large paint brushes. The procession stopped outside the cookhouse and dining room building and after some measuring painted on the wall the words BUCKINGHAM PALACE.

The Welsh Guards' Warrant Officer turned out to be a Drill Sergeant (known throughout lower ranks a 'Drill Pig') who had come to assist our RSM with the procedure required for guard mount at the Palace, although I doubt if our RSM needed too much assistance as he'd also been in the Guards at one time. While this was going on and we were given a break I noticed a group of men paraded on the veranda of the Orderly Room and purely by chance I heard someone call out, 'Group No 76, parade for release! Sir!'

As I've mentioned, I was allocated to that group with the suffix DR (Deferred Regular). To see these men parade for the last time did make me wonder if I had done the right thing.

Oh, well. *Nil Desperandum*!

Drill and procedures went on apace under the Welsh Guards WO, also under our new RSM, who, we soon found, was no stranger to the world or ways of the Brigade. This new RSM (known as Rocky) turned out to be hard but fair. He would explain and /or demonstrate what he wanted, then allow the men to give the answer. It was not long before he gained the respect of most of the battalion, which was to last long after he had left. In fact he is still talked about at reunions today.

It was discovered that Rocky had devised the new Light Infantry drill which we now practised for so many hours. It is interesting to note that the drill used with the new SA80 assault rifle had its birth in the drill devised by Rocky Knight.

The Band was requested to attend a camp being held by the Shropshire Army Cadet Force near Harlech, North Wales. In those days the railways were helpful and very efficient and the Band were allocated a goods wagon for all their kit and equipment. This wagon was attached to the rear of the train taking us to Ruabon, where we were to change trains but once again the railways came up trumps. When we had alighted from the train at Ruabon, our goods wagon was shunted into sidings to await the train taking us to Harlech. We were thankful for this as the boxes containing the music and equipment were made of solid teak in India and were very heavy indeed.

On arrival at the camp area we discovered that our accommodation was of the tented variety, pitched in a field facing Cardigan Bay. (Today this area has been built upon in a style devised by some Minister or other and dubbed 'Legoland'). After settling in, some of us decided to take a walk into Harlech proper. There was not a lot to keep our attention so we decided to visit a local hostelry and take a drink or two.

We were sitting, chatting at one of the tables when a local youth, (who, we later found out, was always looking for trouble) came over and started asking all the usual questions: 'Where were we from?', 'What are you doing here?' and so on, then started poking fun at our group. Most of us ignored him but three took exception so we decided to leave. The gentlemen's toilet was outside the building and the lads thought it might be an idea to pay a call before setting off back to our camp. Unknown to them, the local provocatuer was already inside. A fairly hefty scuffle ensued and judging by the outcome the odds of three to one were just too much for the local funny boy.

After the matter had been settled we thought it a fair idea to walk back to camp along the sea shore. As we started along the beach it began to rain and as we found out in this part of the country it can not only rain very heavily, but do so for a long time. In fact, it rained almost continuously while we were in Harlech. As the whole camp was tented there was nowhere to get one's things really dry, and although I'd brought both Best and 2nd Best BDs, I travelled back to Wrexham in a boiler suit I had to borrow from the 2nd Battalion, and I wasn't the only one!

On our return to the Battalion, we carried out various drill and manoeuvres necessary for the role we were to play next. The Battalion had been re-organised into three companies, A, C, and HQ, to enable us to carry out the various guards and pickets as required for Royal Duties. At this time the band included twenty-one boys and ex-boys and this despite the loss of one to the Grenadier Guards ('claimed' by his elder brother), two to the Parachute Regiment, and one to the bugle platoon, plus several others for various reasons.

The Band and Bugles were paraded for yet another inspection, this time to have our anklets (gaiters) checked for any wear or fraying. These were exchanged where necessary but I had my doubts as to whether or not any person, military or civilian, was going to crawl around on the floor to look that closely at this particular piece of our equipment. On the other hand considering the importance of Royal Duties, I suppose it was necessary. The one thing I do know was that those who had an exchange had a lot of work, not only to get their gaiters up to 'snow white' quickly, but also to get the straps up to a black polished surface in time for the first mount.

A P Sisley

The move from Wrexham was made *en masse* by train from Wrexham station to Addison Road station (adjacent to Earls Court in London). On detraining, the Battalion formed up in column with the Band and Bugles at the head. The order to march was given and we set off at a rather sedate, Heavy Infantry pace. Our route took us along the Thames Embankment to Chelsea, passing the main gate of the Royal Hospital where, having heard our approach, the Chelsea Pensioners lined the pavement and applauded as we passed.

As we approached the barracks we quickened the pace to our Light Infantry rate (140 paces per minute, although we often exceeded that). Chelsea barracks at that time were entered through a gateway with the CO's office on the left, the main guard room on the right and straight ahead an archway leading on to the square.

At this time the Scots Guards were paraded on the square prior to their handing over for their departure to Tripoli. What they must have thought when this flying mass shot through the archway I can only guess.

As one of the band storemen it was my responsibility to make sure that our stores arrived in the right room. So while the rest of the band were getting settled into their first floor barrack room I had the none-to-easy task of making sure that the stores being handled by duty men were being put in the places required by my superiors – none-to-easy, as the men felt somewhat aggrieved having also been on the march in.

To make matters a little more difficult, the Band Sergeant decided he wanted to bunk in the stores so, as the boxes came through the door, he instructed the men to arrange them to form two walls of his bunk, just inside the stores door. The l/corporal and I made ourselves comfortable at the end of the stores, farthest from the door and nearest to the fire place.

Chelsea Barracks had been built prior to the Crimean War and I'm sure that very little had been changed since. The barrack blocks, one either side of the entrance archway, consisted of ground floor rooms, one on each side of a central entrance, and two first floor rooms reached via a concrete stairway situated in the centre entrance. There were ablutions on each floor The room the band occupied had an NCO's bunk on the head of the stairs, on this occasion occupied by the RSM. This, of course, led to all sorts of comment but in the main worked out very well and our lives were fairly quiet, especially when Royal Duties commenced.

When the duties formed up, they did so as follows: Right to

left with their backs to the barrack block. The Buckingham Palace Detachment, St. James' Palace Detachment, Windsor Castle Detachment, the Band and Bugles paraded opposite the guards with their backs to the NAAFI and facing the guards. One of the duties for the Officer of the Day was to inspect the Band and Bugles while the Adjutant inspected the guards.

One particular day the Orderly Officer was a rather young subaltern who on reaching the place in our ranks occupied by a very long-serving l/corporal, looked him over, until he lighted on his medal ribbons.

'Isn't your General Service Medal in the wrong place?'

Without a moment's hesitation the l/corporal replied, 'I got mine in '36 not '46!'

Inspections over, we set forth through the rear gate to be met by our escort, a member of the Metropolitan Police. As we shot out of the gate the constable looked quite ashen, but being a London Bobby, he quickly weighed up the situation and from somewhere produced a bicycle and was thus able to keep a little ahead of us to control the traffic at the various junctions we had to cross. On the occasion of our next mount we were escorted by a mounted police constable, but even he wasn't too happy.

'I've just got my horse used to the Foot Guards,' he observed, 'and now you lot have to show up!'

The first mount was quite interesting from various points of view, as not only was it the first time we wore green berets (which made a large number of the crowd think we were commandos) but it was also the first time we showed off the new Light Infantry drill to the public, as well as the Guards.

All went well with the mount and it was really quite amusing, especially when various persons who were obviously knowledgeable on the matter of guard mounts voiced their views loudly.

'They've got it all wrong!'

However, they quickly realised they were witnessing something new and quite different. The RSM was on hand to see nothing went wrong and I'm sure there was not one man on parade who would not have chosen to do an extended period of extra duties rather than feel the wrath of Rocky. There was little chance of our getting anything wrong.

As was the custom, the mounting band provides the incidental music while the 1st Reliefs were posted. The most vivid occasion that comes to mind was the day Prince Charles was born. I recall one of the pieces of music played on that day was *The Marriage of Figaro*. My mind always goes back to that day whenever I hear it played.

At this time the sentry boxes were outside the railings and on this day the change-over took a little longer than usual. As is the pattern when the old guard have departed to their barracks the St James' detachment with the regimental colours march out to St James Palace, leaving the Buckingham Palace detachment *in situ*. With the Brigade of Guards this part of the ceremony is carried out by The Corps of Drums/Pipes and Drums but unfortunately for us, both the Band and Bugles had to accompany this part of the mount and dismount.

With the guard and the colours safely tucked away in the

guard room, the band and buglers marched (not playing) back to Chelsea Barracks, while the Guards had only to march across the road to Wellington Barracks.

On the route we took in both directions, a newspaper seller we passed would always, without fail, hold up the latest edition so we could read the headlines.

A little farther along the road was a pub called *The Bag o' Nails*, which we very quickly learned was a haunt of homosexuals who plied the soldiers with drink in an attempt to bend them to their ways. I can honestly say, right up to this day, I prefer my liaisons to be wearing skirts, and female!

On our return to barracks the first thing we did on being dismissed was to hurtle to our barrack rooms and re-blanco belts and gaiters, as well as polish boots and instruments. We were lucky to have this time before our midday meal, otherwise it would have taken up precious time in the evening.

Two weeks after we'd arrived, the other half of the barracks was occupied by The Middlesex Regiment which lightened the load quite a lot, in fact cut the guard mounts by at least a third. I may be making everything sound easy and perfect but I can assure you it was not. I recall one incident when the buglers (all sixteen of them) had to sound the Officers Call, which was the signal for officers to join their guards. The buglers sounded but no officers appeared.

It so happened that the adjutant was on the square and he instructed the bugle major to sound the call again, once again with no response. The adjutant is to the officers what the RSM is to the other ranks, and this one was becoming bad tempered. On four occasions he told the buglers to sound but still received no response from the direction of the Officers' Mess. We didn't mind; it took the heat away from us. He stormed across the square, into the Officers' Mess from which after a very few moments the offending officers, hastily adjusting their dress, erupted like bullets from a gun.

The guilty officers were awarded extra guards and duties but what exactly their punishment was I cannot say, though I can guess it wasn't light. The only incidence of lateness for duty within the band was due to two bandsmen who lived out and, with the change of clocks to British Summer Time, forgot to alter theirs! They got off with a severe ear bashing from the CO.

One morning just after reveille there came a loud knocking on the stores door which I answered to find the Orderly Sergeant standing outside with the Orderly Officer beside him, gazing at his watch, obviously timing how long it would be before anyone climbed out of their bed and opened the door. They entered the stores and found the Band Sergeant in his bunk and the l/corporal in his bed at the far end of the stores. The Orderly Officer and Sergeant could not say a word about me as I had opened the door, and thus he couldn't prove that I'd remained in my bed after reveille. The two NCOs received a right rocketing.

A couple of days later I was informed by the bandmaster that I was to find a bed space in the Band barrack room since my duties as a storeman were no longer required. (It does not take an Einstein to work out why.) If the two NCOs had used their brains and moved themselves out of their beds when they heard the knocking, all would have been well. I was not particularly worried about it, although my relationship with these NCOs was rather guarded for some time.

In the band at this time there were several unusual individuals, among them was a Corporal who was a devout Christian, in fact so much so that after his discharge he became an Army Bible Reader for many years right up to his death a couple of years ago.

Another character in our ranks was one who was into everything, including cutting the RSM's hair, though none of us can remember seeing any money changing hands. In the MT section was a dispatch rider who came from South London and seemed able to get hold of any and every item others might want. One day I was standing at the top of the stairwell in the barrack block when he came in and without hesitation asked me if I could make use of a set of cutlery. I was a little taken aback but thought I could, if the price was right.

He rapidly informed me that £10.00 would see me in possession of a complete twelve place set of cutlery. The next day he appeared with a cardboard box in which was the cutlery, as described, with each piece individually wrapped in tissue paper. I handed over the money then dispatched the cutlery to my home to await the day I would be able to make use of it. (Some pieces of this electro-plated-nickel cutlery were still in service as late as 1977.)

The 14th September saw the battalion providing a Guard of Honour in the inner quadrangle of Buckingham Palace, when King George opened Parliament. On his return the King inspected the guard, as well as the Band and Bugles. Her Majesty the Queen seemed also to take a great interest, which I could only put down to the fact that she was Colonel-in-Chief of the King's Own Yorkshire Light Infantry, a post she held from the day she married the then Duke of York. (Her Majesty was subsequently appointed Colonel-in-Chief of the new Light Infantry upon its formation in 1962 and held this position until her death.)

Some may consider it old-fashioned, but I was not the only one on parade that day to feel a thrill of pride to be so near to our King and Queen.

On 26th October the battalion provided troops for the lining of The Mall on the occasion of the State Opening of Parliament. The Band and Bugles were on parade and, having brought the troops to their position, had to provide entertaining music for the crowds and play the National Anthem whenever the procession passed. The band formed a circle with the buglers forming an inner circle, their duty being to hold the music as required. All went well until the Royal Horse Artillery commenced their Forty-One Gun salute. Every time a gun fired the buglers would jump about six inches, so we lost our place on the music. We were annoyed at the time but had a good laugh afterwards.

A P Sisley

During one of the breaks in the ceremonies I felt a tap on my shoulder and, looking round, found my old school headmaster standing there. It seemed he was in London to attend some conference or other and had made the time to come and watch his old regiment in which he'd served as a driver during the First World War. This was the last time I was to see 'Titch' Northern but I remember him with much affection and still recall what he wrote in my autograph book when I left school. It was almost as if he knew I was destined to become a military musician: 'Don't be sharp; don't be flat; be natural.' Only instead of the words, he had used the musical symbols.

Another incident that took place that day caused much amusement among us but not for those affected. As this day was a Battle Honour day the colours being carried had to be dressed with an Immortal. An Immortal was a laurel wreath attached to the crown at the top of the pike staff to which the colours were fixed. This solemn duty was performed by the bugle major before we left barracks. Nothing untoward happened until the Royal procession returned down The Mall. The troops presented arms, we played the National Anthem, the colours dipped, and off fell the Immortal! It rolled off down the Mall until stopped by a member of the Metropolitan Police who returned the offending article to the officer carrying the colours, who, in turn, directed him to the bugle major.

There were certainly some red faces but nothing much was said. It was looked upon as just one of those things. 'But don't let it happen again!'

A SHROPSHIRE BOY

We were still receiving re-enforcements – ours in the form of Buglers and a CSM of some stature from the Somerset LI. This CSM had obviously been a boxer in his time and, as we learned later, also held the championship for throwing the cricket ball. (Ever tried it? We did and it ain't easy!) The CSM took over the duties of bass drummer, and we must have been the only band at the time with a WO2 (CSM) doing this job, and he did a very fine job, although on more than one occasion split the drum skin (sometimes by request!). The drum skins in those days were real animal skins not the plastic used today, therefore were affected by rain and cold.

Another CSM to affect us directly was the CSM of Head Quarter Company, who carried the nick name 'Birdie', due to his habit of calling every one 'Bird'. This habit caused an incident of some humour – at least, so we thought.

A new draft had just been allocated their companies and Birdie was taking the particulars of the newcomers. He arrived in front of one of the lads.

'What's your name, Bird?'

'Parrot. Sir!'

It seems that The Bird was not in too good a humour and repeated the question twice more and on receiving the same answer on both occasions placed the lad in the guard room on a charge of insolence. The matter was sorted out by none other than the Provost Sergeant, Paddy who had sorted out the matter of my stripes, so the lad – Private Parrot – joined the company, with which he served for some time, but admitted later he'd wondered at first what sort of battalion he was joining.

A P Sisley

One evening the battalion received an emergency call from one of the hospitals asking for volunteers to give blood. Their blood bank had been contaminated and they needed replacement as a matter of urgency. I volunteered but as I had never given blood before I was definitely apprehensive. The needles they used in those days were knitting needles compared to those in use today but I was young, and the smile of a pretty nurse worked wonders. I continued to give blood for some time but sadly, owing to the medication I take these days, mine is no longer acceptable.

During off-duty periods we were able to make use of the facilities offered by the Nuffield Club. This was situated behind St Martin-in-the-Fields church. Besides offering all the usual comforts (tea, coffee and sandwiches at very cheap rates) you could also obtain tickets for all the London theatres, available most evenings about an hour before curtain up.

One evening, having obtained tickets for a show, a friend and I were hurrying along when we came across a small crowd of people standing so as to block the pavement. My friend and I pushed our way through and as we did so we bumped into a very attractive lady.

I caught up with my friend. 'Did you know who that was?' I asked him.

'No.'

'Jean Simmons!' I said, and it was.

He nearly dropped to the ground in a dead faint.

A SHROPSHIRE BOY

Another evening found us outside the BBC Radio studios in New Bond Street where, purely by chance, there was an ex-member of the regiment (old India) on door duty. He invited us in to listen and watch a rehearsal that was taking place. It was quite an experience and we took advantage of his invitation to go back any time he was on duty.

To see some of the people who up to that time had only been voices on the radio really was worth the effort to get there when they were either rehearsing or even broadcasting.

Nearer to the barracks was a pub called *The Rose and Crown* and on occasion after Sunday lunch my friend from Hereford, his brother and I would take a pint or two, depending on the state of our finances. We would then make our way to the boating lake in Battersea Park, hire a craft each and set off across the lake. There were many collisions and rammings, as well as threats that we would be banned from the lake, though I think the man in charge liked us really and these threats were never carried through.

I'm fairly sure that the rules governing Royal Duties state that overcoats will be worn, regardless of the weather, from October through to April. The Band and Bugles paraded in overcoats for inspection by the Quarter Master. The QM arrived with a tailor in tow. The tailor was carrying a rod upon which a white band had been painted The rod was placed against the overcoat and if there was any discrepancy regarding length of an overcoat it would be handed in for shortening if too long or exchange if too short. Everyone had to have new buttons bearing the regimental crest. I was one of the lucky ones in that I had to exchange therefore the tailors had to replace the buttons The finished product certainly was impressive as, despite the height of each individual, every coat was the same height from the ground. I often wondered about the expense incurred in this operation, but as long as we were on Royal Duties, cost apparently was not a factor.

There was yet another measuring parade! This time it was to provide the Band and Bugles with pre-1939 uniforms, consisting of 'red' jackets, dark blue trousers, with thin red piping down the seams, and a rifle green peaked cap. After returning to our barrack rooms to get into these articles, we paraded again for inspection by the Quarter Master He asked every man in turn if he felt comfortable. Most of us replied that we were, until he reached a certain trombone player.

'These trousers feel like the dance hall across the road,' he was told.

The QM looked a little puzzled. 'There's no dance hall across the road.'

'That's right,' the bandsman replied. 'No ballroom!'

The QM took it in good part but, although there was some truth in the trombonist's complaint, I don't recall the trousers being changed.

During our tour of duty two films were made in which members of the battalion appeared. The first was entitled *Adam and Evelyn*, in which a shot was taken from between a persons knees across the road towards the Palace just as the old guard were slow marching away to barracks.

The other film was *A Run for Your Money* which showed the adventures of two Welshmen up in London for an International Rugby match. The scene took in the changing of the guard at the Tower of London, and had to be filmed a number of times. That didn't worry the lads too much as I believe they faired rather well that night. The film was shown on television recently and I wonder how many of the guard are still around? I know that the son of one of the officers who was with us at this time carried out the duty of guard commander at the Tower during a recent tour of duty by the present day Light Infantry.

As is always the case with Royal duties by those other than the Brigade, very few got leave over the Christmas period, so much of the 'Entertainment' was home made. To help things along the irrepressible Rocky appeared in the dining room at lunch time.

'Today is your day,' he announced. 'The other three hundred and sixty four are mine. ENJOY!'

Whereupon he placed a pint glass of beer on his head and invited the men to knock it off. Despite an absolute shower of bread rolls, oranges, and apples, no one succeeded!

At this time I was walking out with a young lady working in the NAAFI who was waiting for a posting overseas. It so happened that her home was in Barnet which was in easy reach by underground train (which in those days provided a service even on Christmas Day). I was invited to spend what was left of the day with her and her family and the one thing I remember clearly was being able to sit in an arm chair in front of an open fire and not having to think that anyone else might want to join you on the end of a Form, GS. There were fires in the barrack rooms but to get within effective range of it, you always seemed to be waiting for someone else to get up from the Form, GS.

I should mention two other members of the band. One was the drummer who used to clatter away for hours on his practice pad and earned himself the nickname *Woodpecker*. The other chap was always late. When the drummer was getting married and invited any of the band who cared to attend to the reception. On the day, some of us were getting dressed in our best uniforms, polishing our brasses and removing the dust from our shoes when we noticed that the chap who was always late was nowhere near ready. A decision was made for the rest of us to go on to Waterloo Station. The train we were supposed to catch was in the platform awaiting the signal to depart when we arrived at the barrier but the 'Job'sworth' ticket collector refused to let us through without a ticket.

Off to the ticket office we went, bought our tickets and returned to the barrier just in time to see our train disappearing out of the station. There was nothing for it but to wait for the next available train to Godalming. On arrival at our destination we alighted from the train to be greeted by the 'wayward one', whom we had left in the barracks. How on earth he got there, we never found out.

The drummer obtained his discharge by purchase while we were in Hong Kong and went on to join a well known quartet and for a long time could be heard every Tuesday morning in a radio programme called *Music Box*. Their name, I regret, has been lost to me with the passing of time.

The tardy bandsman who'd beat us to the wedding also had a habit of coming in after everyone else was asleep, and invariably disturbed them, so some of the bandsmen decided to play a prank on him They stuffed a suit of denims (working dress) to look like a human and suspended it over his bed. Thinking that not enough, they lifted the very ancient cast iron coal box, which had *VR* cast on its side, on to his bed. When he came in the wayward one, seeing this heap, decided to sleep on the floor. On awakening in the morning, this monument had to be removed. The wayward one helped and started to remove the coal box which, being old and worn, decided enough was enough and its bottom split. Coal dust burst downwards and outwards.

We spent the hour or so before inspection trying to remove coal dust from every nook and cranny. *'The biter bit,'* one could say.

In every regiment there is always one. Ours was a particular Colour Sergeant, who whenever he was on barrack guard tried to make everyone's life a misery! When you presented yourself at the guardroom to book out you found a 6' Form, GS, placed approximately four feet in front of the table at which sat the Colour Sergeant. You halted at the form and waited to be summoned forward. Heaven help the soldier foolish enough to present himself between the form and the table. To say the least, you began to doubt your parentage. After what seemed an eternity, you were beckoned forward for a minute inspection, from your cap badge, down through your tie knot, your belt and trouser crease to your shoes. (And in winter months you would be told to remove your overcoat so this inspection could be carried out.)

If he was then satisfied he would enter your details in the booking out book but you still had to leave his presence in a smart manner otherwise you would be called back to receive a lecture on moving in a soldierly manner. In my case, the young lady whom I mentioned earlier, having finished work, would be waiting, usually in the cold, for me to walk her back to her residence. The procedure was repeated upon your return and I'm afraid to admit that if you wanted SPD (Sober and Properly Dressed) written against your name, you went along with his little game.

On guard mount or dismount, it was the usual procedure for the band to place their march cards in order before they paraded. The system worked well unless two people – the bandmaster and the Band Sergeant – gave a different card order. One day returning to barracks with the dismounting guard we were given the order, 'Change cards!'

The movement was carried out but when the band started to play. half the band struck up with one march and the other half with a different march. To compound the fracas, the buglers were completely at a loss!

The command was given again: 'Change cards!'

The result? Each half of the band started to play the march the other half had been playing! Thundering double taps were given on the Bass Drum and the word passed from the bandmaster as to which march would be played, and peace reigned.

While on the subject of marches I remember on one dismount after we had slow marched out of the Palace gates we struck up with *Sambre et Meuse*, a French march, much to the delight of a group of French Officer Cadets who were on exchange and had been watching the guard mount.

At this time, the Army was paying a bounty to any man who re-enlisted to encourage trained men to come back into the ranks. One of these re-enlistments said he'd been a cornet player in the Royal Marines. He was accepted, kitted out, received his bounty and promptly disappeared!

Salute The Soldier Week was still with us but much on the wane. Nevertheless, the powers-that-be thought it would be a good public relations exercise if the band put in an appearance on the steps of Hammersmith Town Hall in aid of such a week. During the performance I committed the cardinal sin – I DROPPED A WIND IRON! – the first time ever.

As it was an unpaid performance the BM could not dock a fine from my performance money, but I did get a serious telling off when we got back to barracks.

One night soon after this, someone broke into the NAAFI (in the Nissen Hut across the square from the barrack blocks and not too difficult to break in), removed all the cigarettes and placed them in the back of a 15cwt truck parked near by. One can only assume the thieves were going to come back later and remove their ill-gotten gains later but unfortunately for them, they'd chosen the vehicle that was the duty vehicle used to take the Orderly Officer around the various guards and duties at Buckingham Palace, St James' Palace, The Tower of London and the Bank of England. It was learned later that both the officer and the driver were out of cigarettes and had been scrounging a smoke wherever they went.

When the break in was discovered in the morning and the SIB (Special Investigation Branch, Royal Military Police) started nosing around, leading to the discovery of the contents and load of the 15cwt, a quiet chuckle was had by quite a few.

The band was booked to play at the Shropshire Show, to be held just outside Shrewsbury and would be required to provide the music for the performance of the Kings Troop Royal Horse Artillery who would giving a display at the show. As we were in London already it was decided that we would attend a rehearsal by the Kings Troop on their training ground, which was situated between Regents Park and the Regent's Canal. I had played in this area as a child and to visit it again made me thoughtful. The rehearsal was very interesting but I do admit that being so near those very mobile horses and gun carriages with no brakes made one very wary.

In April 1949, our tour of Royal Duties came to an end. By this time we could tell which of the Guards bands was on duty. One in particular was the band of the Irish Guards, (in time to have as their director, Jimmy Jaeger, at this time bandmaster of the Middlesex, our opposite numbers), whose euphonium player sounded as though he were on a platform above the rest, so beautiful was the sound he produced!

Our duty done, the battalion marched out on the reverse route we had marched in. We set off at a cracking pace but it was not long before the RSM came forward to the bugle major.

'What the hell are you doing? Trying to kill the battalion? Slow down to a moderate pace!'

As the battalion were wearing Field Marching Order which consisted of Large Pack (full), Small Side Pack (full), Pouches (full), Water Bottle , plus personal weapons, there was no doubt they'd had a slog for no reason.

At Addison Road Station the battalion boarded a train while the Band and Bugles climbed aboard two Luton furniture vans to be transported to the Household Cavalry Barracks, Windsor. The move was to provide some 'swank' to the guards being undertaken by one of the companies of the battalion.

Most of Windsor is inclined up towards the castle, and the march there always left most of us gasping, so by the time we reached the guard room we were nearly on our chin straps!

Our duties in Windsor done we rejoined the battalion in Wing Barracks, near Bulford, Wiltshire. The barracks received its name from its close association with the Airborne troops that trained in that area and this association was being carried on through a 'greasy spoon' café run by an ex-Paratrooper who had seen the potential of such an establishment during his service there. (It turned out he was right, and was doing very nicely.)

A SHROPSHIRE BOY

CHAPTER FOUR

Away, take heed; I will abroad.

In our ranks at this time was a bandsman whose reputation as a distance runner was burgeoning. He often declared in no uncertain terms that he would not be going abroad with us, or anybody else! This chap was always going away at weekends to take part in some long-distance race or other, although this was in the days before the Marathon had achieved its current popularity.

One Saturday morning he announced that he was to run in a Marathon that afternoon and away he went. We thought no more about it until he had not returned by the following Tuesday. It was only as we were preparing his kit to be handed into stores that we discovered that every time he went running he had taken some article that would be of use to him when he went 'on the trot'. We never saw hide nor hair of him again. Maybe one day he will say 'Hello'.

The Band Sergeant who had joined us in Shrewsbury left us rather suddenly and his place was taken by a sergeant who had been through Kneller Hall but had not passed out as bandmaster. He and I were to cross swords on many occasions, although I never really discovered why that should be. It just turned out that way.

The occasion for wearing our 'red' tunics at last came to pass. We were informed that besides our appearance at the Shrewsbury Show, we would be providing the music for an inspection of the ATS girls stationed in the area, by their Commandant, The Princess Royal. Of course there had to be rehearsals as the girls had little or no experience of marching to a band. These rehearsals were held in the Depot under the gentle guiding hand of the Depot RSM.

It was entertaining to listen to the RSM biting back his words every time he was about to yell at one of the girls over some misdemeanour, saying instead, 'Now, Ladies'. It must have been quite a strain for him.

Rehearsals completed, the actual parade took place on the green inside the walls of Shrewsbury Castle and the girls acquitted themselves very well. After the inspection the parade marched through the streets in the centre of town to the applause of many of the town's citizens.

We also attended the Shropshire Show but had to make some changes to the music accompanying the Musical Drive by the Kings Troop as during a rehearsal two of the guns had turned over due to the overnight rain, leaving the grass surface very greasy. Luckily none of the horses or drivers were hurt.

Throughout the period that the battalion was preparing for service overseas the band were still carrying out public concerts and engagements, the most memorable of which was a week's appearance on the promenade at Bognor Regis.

The band was housed in the Depot of the Royal Sussex Regiment in Chichester which meant an early start each morning so as to be ready for the afternoon performance. This did not please everyone and there was a fair amount of grumbling going on.

However, to keep the workload down, the bandmaster, who was a wily bird, would address the audience after every performance.

'If any one has a favourite piece of music they would like to hear, would they write it on a piece of paper and hand it to either myself or the Band Sergeant and it will be placed with any others to form a gala concert on Saturday evening.'

Nothing unusual, you might say, but when you consider that the visitors 'changed over' on Saturdays, it meant the majority of those he had addressed would have gone home so would not know whether we played their selection or not. Those who had stayed would be informed that the requests had been so numerous it had been impossible to include them all. As far as we were concerned we played the rehearsed programme and breathed a sigh of relief.

In due course we received our booster inoculations, and were issued with sea kit bags, plus all sorts of tropical gear. The ribald comments that were passed the first time we tried on our *shorts, tropical* are not really fit to repeat!

One item we all wondered about was the withdrawal of all white towels which were replaced by green ones. This mystery was explained when we learned that during the Second World War the soldiers' habit of tucking their towels into their shirt collars and letting the rest hang down their backs while they carried out their ablutions could be sighted by enemy artillery spotters from quite a distance, resulting in shelling, which in turn caused casualties.

The small sea kit bag was packed with all you would need during the voyage while your normal kit bag would be marked with the company colours and stowed in the ship's hold. HQ colours were red and green and remained on my kit bag to the day I handed it in on discharge.

The band were instructed they would be required to wear their overcoats in bandoleer fashion for the journey from Bulford to the troop ship. I have never understood the reasoning behind this instruction because once we had boarded the transport we had neither use nor space for them.

We boarded HMT *The Empress of Australia* from the same Liverpool dock from which we'd played in the 1st battalion home some eighteen months before. The band were directed to occupy 'E' deck, which was down in the bowels of the ship, or at least so it seemed at the time! We were issued with a hammock which was wrapped around two blankets held together by a length of twine. We were told that our hammock and blankets would be tied in this fashion every morning and stowed in the designated rack before inspection.

One of the first things I did was to hunt out the ship's carpenter and beg two pieces of wood 18" long and 1" wide into which I persuaded the chippie to cut a notch at each end. I'd read somewhere that this was the best way to keep the ends of ones hammock open, making it a lot easier to get in or out. It certainly worked for me.

On the way to the chippies, I came across the ship's bakery and learned that the bakers made their own bread rolls and any surplus was made available to any passengers requiring them. I also found out that it was possible to obtain a slice of cold cooked meat from the ship's galley. This, eaten in the open air with a fresh bread roll seemed to stave off the *mal-de mer*. It certainly worked for me.

While on the subject of *mal-de-mer*, one of our buglers had only to look at sea water to be terribly sick. On the first day he disappeared not to show his face for some days. We discovered that he'd taken refuge in a storage locker.

Every meal time the duty representative would collect the meal for the mess. I vividly remember that one day when the sea was running a little rough, the duty bandsman appeared at the top of the companion way and started to descend when the ship ploughed rather deeply into a trough. The man lost his footing and landed on his back at the bottom of the steps. The 'dixie' he had been carrying went up in the air, resulting in the contents pouring all over his prostrate body. Luckily the contents were not all that hot, otherwise it could have been nasty. Everybody started to laugh, as one seems inclined to do on these occasions but we soon stopped when we realised it was our meal, and the chances of getting it replaced were almost nil!

Amongst the items issued was Salt Water Soap. This was to be used for washing and showering, as fresh water was at a premium and only to be used for medicinal purposes and drinking. Like thousands of others, I never could raise a lather using this soap.

It was over the matter of fresh water that the new Band Sergeant and I crossed swords for the first (and certainly not the last) time. The drinking water tank on the mess deck had a very stale smell while the water had a musty taint. It was decided to empty and re-fill the tank. Being mess orderly for the day I got the job. While I was so engaged I noticed that the other bandsmen had disappeared and as I discovered later had been called to the upper deck for a lesson in the *Elements of Music* given by the Band Sergeant. When I realised the situation I finished off and made my way to the upper deck to join the rest. The Sergeant wasn't too happy, which I could understand, but he kept having a dig.

I undoubtedly made things worse by asking, 'Is fresh water

less important than the *Elements of Music*?'

The Sergeant 'took off' and said he would see me later. Luckily for me he never seemed to find the time. I found out later that I would have been better off if I had stayed away from the lesson as the Sergeant had not noticed my absence until I arrived to join the class but he didn't forget, as was to be proved at a later date.

Our journey took us through the Straits of Gibraltar and as the weather became hotter we were given permission to sleep on the open decks, provided we moved before the Lascars started to wash down the decks in the early mornings. Most of the Lascars would shout before turning on the hoses but there were occasions when I'm sure they did not and I was suddenly aware of water streaming past my nose as I lay on the deck. The Lascars took great delight in watching us trying to rescue our hammocks before they got soaked through.

The ship eventually docked in Port Said. I say docked, though in fact she was tied up at the end of a pontoon. Permission was given to those wishing to go ashore, provided they were properly dressed, i.e.: Shorts, Shirts and Hose tops. On leaving the ship we walked over the pontoon on which I am sure thousands, if not millions, had walked before us. The few hours ashore certainly eased out the creases. We returned to the ship to join in the time honoured tradition of bargaining with the 'bum' boats, as they and our ancestors had done for many a year before us. The *Gili-Gili* man (a magician) came aboard, again as was the custom, and as always made fools of everyone with his tricks. On looking back the way British soldiers behaved towards the Arab traders was uncalled for and at times down right disgusting! I very much doubt if it would be tolerated today. However, the arabs weren't always on the losing side and could pull the wool when they put their minds to it.

There were boys who swam alongside the ship and dived for coins thrown over the side. Very often they would dive down, rise to the surface with their arm raised above their heads, their fist clenched, indicating they had a coin in it. This seemed to encourage the troops to throw even more coins which meant the boys had even more chances to retrieve our money.

A popular song at the time was *I'd like to get you on a slow boat to China*, although I feel it was not the most popular among those on board our ship, for this was our destination – at least, the British colony of Hong Kong. After Port Said, our journey continued through the Suez Canal and sometimes in the still of the night a voice would ring out, 'Get your knees brown!' To which some long-served old sweat might reply, 'This is my third time, not my first. Get some in!'

Just after we had entered the Red Sea the ship was stopped while a service was held to commit one of the ship's engineering officers, who had died, to a watery grave. The silence of a ship lying absolutely still, broken only by the whirring of the essential fans is a most eerie sensation which I shall never forget.

Our next port of call was Aden and once again we were allowed shore leave. At one point I was stood in the darkness watching the local craftsmen at work and had the sensation of somebody standing behind me. I looked round and found a 'fuzzy wuzzy' standing at my shoulder. My Father had spoken many times of these noble warriors and it was quite a shock to find one so close in the twilight without any warning. I felt no fear but knowing that he'd come so close certainly gave me food for thought.

As we sailed on we passed a French troop ship loaded to the gunnels with French Foreign Legionnaires, presumably on their way to Indo China. They attempted to make contact across the gap between the two vessels until silenced by their NCOs. I wonder how many survived that bloody campaign?

As we approached Colombo in Ceylon (now Sri Lanka), I witnessed a rather strange phenomenon. The ship was about twelve miles out when those on deck saw a brown cloud travelling across the surface of the sea The cloud was of such density that it even obscured the sun. When it reached the ship we realised that it was a sand storm and disappeared from the open decks rather fast! It was said later that it was very unusual that far out to sea.

While the ship was at sea various activities took place, ranging from PT to firing live ammunition from the Bren guns at various targets thrown over the side into the sea. The afternoon activities consisted of deck games or Housey-Housey (Bingo), which was the only legal gambling pastime allowed in the services. There were also quite a few *Crown and Anchor* cloths laid out. The man running the game would have got hold of a square of white cloth, marked up the squares with the requisite 'Crowns' and 'Anchors' then set up shop in some quiet corner with one or two mates keeping watch for NCOs or ship's police. If anyone in authority was spotted, the cloth would be swept up in a single motion and placed beneath the banker's backside. There were also plenty of card schools (but we only played for matches!).

The battalion were encouraged to remove their shirts as the CO felt that a little sunburn now was better than being unable to wear equipment later. It turned out to be a wise decision.

It was also decided that the band, as stretcher bearers, should receive some training. Therefore a series of lectures on basic first aid would be given by the Medical Officer. The MO decided to hold his talks on the very top deck of the ship, which meant we had to pass through the deck where the ladies had chosen to do their sun bathing; I've never known men to drag their feet so much!

The MO was able to hold our attention long enough to get the basics of the subject over to most of us. Then came the crunch! Questions on how to treat an injured person were asked. All went well until the MO came to a bandsman who had been only half listening and really wasn't too interested in the proceedings.

Tourniquets were still very much in use at that time and would be placed between the wound and the heart. The MO asked this chap how he would treat a severe head wound.

After a few moments thought the bandsman replied.

'Place a tourniquet around his neck, maintain pressure until the patient turned blue then release it but repeat as and when, remembering to mark the patient's forehead with the letter 'T'.'

The MO went berserk. 'Get out of my sight!' he barked. 'And I hope no one ever has the misfortune to fall into your hands!'

When we reached Singapore, as the ship docked a staff car was seen drawing up to a dais which had been erected on the dockside and the small figure of General Sir John Harding was seen to alight from the car and mount the dais. Sir John then addressed all those who had remained on deck and were interested enough to stay and listen. He delivered his much reported speech.

'If it comes to fighting, fight hard! If it comes to shooting, shoot straight, and shoot to kill!'

Some of the newspapers back home took exception to these exhortations but I feel they were justified a few years later.

During our short time in Singapore some mail caught up with us, and I received my first '*Dear John*' letter. The young lady I'd been walking out with in Chelsea had been posted to East Africa and she'd decided that as the battalion was heading for a three year posting (as was the norm in those days) she really couldn't be fair and say she would wait.

We sailed on the last leg of our journey to Hong Kong. It was during this stage that we learned of the Yangtze Incident, involving *HMS Amethyst*. The battalion were told of the possibility of action almost as soon as we arrived, as it seemed the Chinese Communist were pushing the Nationalist forces out of the country rather quickly and would reach the border sooner rather than later.

As *The Empress of Australia* docked in Hong Kong, our attention was drawn to the very battered and much holed *Amethyst*, tied up directly across from us. She really had taken a beating if the visible damage was anything to go by, but we could only see one side. When the full story was released I am sure many of we pongos mentally took our hats off to the crew.

CHAPTER FIVE

Home, home (be it never so homely.)

We were transported to our future home in 3-ton lorries driven by Chinese drivers of the Royal Army Service Corps. The seething masses of Hong Kong and Kowloon came as a shock to our western eyes. It seemed to us that many of them had a death wish as they crossed the streets in such a manner as to be knocked down nearly every time. But, as we learned later, in their minds, the nearer they got to the vehicle, the more evil spirits following them would be knocked away.

Our convoy wandered its way into a valley which was to be our future home for at least a few months. The tented camp was named after the nearby walled village of Sek Kong. It was surrounded by very steep hills upon one of which was a water pool. This pool was roughly half way up the hill and was fed by water coming down from the crest.

As the days went by we learned to use the pool as an early warning system as to the chances of heavy rain. When the clouds came over the top of the hill the water channel would become very full, making a wonderful waterfall some minutes before the rain hit us. This at least gave us a little time in which to slacken the tent guy ropes. If you didn't, there was the possibility of much toil ahead in re-erecting your tent.

After we'd been in the camp for a couple of days, a typhoon warning was given and we were told to strike our tents and weight everything down. It so happened the band of the Argyll and Sutherland Highlanders were paying a visit to entertain the battalion when they saw what we were doing. They roared with laughter; it seemed that these warnings came and went quite frequently without result. The old stagers simply ignored them, as after that, we also did from time to time.

There was a metalled road along the bottom and up one side of the camp. Alongside the roads were monsoon drains made of concrete, 8' wide at the top opening, and narrowing down to a gulley in the bottom which was about 12" wide and 12" deep. The depth overall was approximately 6' and caught many a man who had imbibed a little too heavily in the canteen. In time we learned that these drains were insufficient to cope with all the storm water but at least did prevent some areas from going under completely.

The Royal Engineer Regiment who had dug and lined the drains as well as erected the few Nissen huts we had, became known as the Whitfield Regiment, owing to the fact that in the course of the work they were plagued by ring worm of quite huge proportions, picked up from the earth. It was discovered that the most effective treatment available at this time was an ointment produced by the Medical Officer stationed in Whitfield Barracks, Kowloon. The only drawback was that the ointment was coloured a bright yellow! The Sappers made quite a pretty picture with their yellow polka dots, although one didn't say so in their hearing.

Another essential task the REs had was to supply water to every military establishment in the colony. Our water was supplied by a large cast iron pipe which had been laid over the hills surrounding the camp. The pipe being open to the air, the water was at least warm. The only snag was that, if one of the Chinese farmers needed more water on his paddy fields, rather than carry water up, he would 'smack' a hole in our supply pipe. This happened quite often despite patrols moving through the area. The repair fell to the REs and wasn't one of their favourite pastimes. Public relations with the locals could be a little strained at times.

We were now part of the 40th Infantry (The Fighting Cocks) Division.

The Division consisted of:

27th Brigade

The Middlesex Regiment

The Royal Leicestershire Regiment

The Argyll and Sutherland Highlanders

28th Brigade

The South Staffordshire Regiment

The Kings Shropshire Light Infantry

The Kings Own Scottish Borderers

29th Brigade

The Cameronians (Scottish Rifles)
The Wiltshire Regiment
The Ghurka Rifles.

Also with us were all the usual ancillaries:
Royal Artillery, Royal Engineers, Ordnance, Medical and Supply Columns.

The fact that we were abroad and fairly wide spread meant that the bugle came into its own again and to help us remember the calls, there were ditties to each one, such as:

Defaulters: 'You can be a defaulter as long as you like, as long as you answer the call!'

Short reveille: 'Charlie, Charlie get out of bed my boy, Charlie, Charlie get out of bed!'

Guard call: 'Come and do a picket boys, come and do a guard. Come and do a picket boys, come and do a guard!'

Cook house: (I doubt that I need to remind anyone of this.)

Sick call: '49, 69, he'll never get there in time. The poor b——s dead!'

Mail call: 'Letter from Lousy Lizzie; letter from Lousy Lou!'

Daily Orders: 'Daily Orders. Daily Orders. Come and see what you've got for tomorrow!'

Officers' Mess Call: 'Officers' wives get puddin' and pie; a soldier's wife gets skilly!'

The King's Shropshire Light Infantry had their own Mess calls which were played on valved bugles. These were taken from French hunting calls and very pretty they sounded.

Band call: 'If you see a band boy kick his bl— y arse!'

General Alarm: 'Sergeant-major's got the horn; Sergeant-major's got the horn!'

Company assembly: 'Company call!' followed by the usual, 'Fall in!'

Fire alarm: 'There's a fire; there's a fire! Come on lads try and put it out!'

Our tents were of Indian manufacture and had a double roof, plus side walls which were rolled back every morning except on Sundays and Holidays. (Holidays came round a little more frequently now, as we were stationed in a British Colony and celebrated their holidays as well as our own.)

The tent area was about 14' square with a floor covering of 2' by 2' concrete slabs. A tent housed six men although some were occupied by eight. Each man had an iron bedstead, blankets and a mosquito net. The mosquito nets were held aloft in all sorts of ways; some tied them to the strings hanging from the inner roof while others were held in place by split bamboo poles tied to the cross head bars of the bed frame.

When the rains came we quickly learned that a drainage ditch was required round the tent to prevent flooding. This seemed simple at first but as we were no drainage engineers we hadn't realised that the ditch needed to be graded to enable the water to be carried away.

The first graded ditch we dug was some nine inches deep at the top end, dropping away towards the next tent. By the time we got to the end of the Company lines the ditch was nearly two feet deep! Some time later the Company lines were moved to allow some work to be carried out and we got caught completely by the rains. It was our own fault; we'd thought it would be a waste of time to dig new drains as the rumour had it that we would be moving back pretty soon.

Sek Kong village itself had a walled house on its outskirts, outside which stood two ornamental cannons. These cannons proved to be too much of a temptation for some of the lads weaving their way back to camp after visiting a local bar and they decided to 'borrow' them. When the matter was reported, all hell broke loose!

Lectures were given about keeping good relations with the locals; not a word about the smashing of the water pipe. Soon after we settled in the Dance band was reformed and it was not long before it was very much in demand to perform in the various Service clubs both in Hong Kong and Kowloon, to say nothing of the numerous Messes and civilian clubs as well as weddings and parties. At this time I had nothing to offer in this direction but admit to feeling a little envious of those who played in the dance band as they were out of camp far more than the rest of us.

The hierarchy thought it would be a good idea for the Division to parade in front of the Governor, at the same time giving the 'watchers' on the Chinese side a glimpse of our Military Might!

The area chosen was alongside our camp so we did not have far to travel, although it did take up time in making sure that the area was spotlessly clean.

At rehearsals there appeared one or two problems caused by the differences between the practices of Heavy and Light Infantry, plus Rifles, generally concerning pace and drill. Most things went well until the march off.

The tank's went past, followed through a cloud of dust by the Heavy Infantry – not bad – then the Light Infantry and Rifles cracked off, which threw the Heavies into confusion. To prevent this confusion on the day, it was decided to leave an interval of some minutes to elapse before we got on the march.

The day arrived; the parade went as planned. However, someone forgot to inform the Governor about this pause in the proceedings, so he and the General Officers on the dais decided that the gap meant the parade was over and started to move around, but when we cracked off, they turned back, tripping over their swords and spurs and their own feet. When we dismissed we had quite a laugh.

From time to time the battalion had to provide guards for Government House also special Guards of Honour.

Government House was situated about a third of the way up the road leading to The Peak on Hong Kong Island. The march up or down was not always welcome. On one occasion the Bass drummer was in hospital suffering appendicitis and his place was taken by the Band Sergeant and half way up the hill there was a mix-up over the signals given on the Bass drum. This put us as a band in a bad light. Nothing was said at the time because I'm sure none of us had any breath to spare!

On our return to camp we had to prepare and lay out our kit for a Brigadier's inspection. As we laid it out, we fell to grumbling as soldiers do and I was in full flow when I looked towards the door space and saw a pair of boots, Hose Tops and gaiters standing outside the tent. Who else but the Band Sergeant! He said nothing other than we were to turn in for band practice immediately after the Brigadier's inspection.

During the inspection an incident took place which I think showed that the inspecting officer was as uninterested as we other ranks were. As always the answer for any missing article of kit or clothing was, as applicable, 'One on, one in the wash, Sir!'

On this occasion the Brigadier reached the bed next to mine and noticed that a pair of gaiters were missing and asked the bandsman concerned where they were. The bandsman replied, "One on, one in the wash, Sir!' The Brigadier moved on without comment but the CO gave the bandsman a long hard stare.

When we had assembled in the practice tent, the Band Sergeant called for silence and informed us that: 'Bandsman Sisley thinks that the recent problems were my fault so we are here to sort it out.'

After this, I thought that was the end of the matter but a few days on found me facing the Company Commander across his desk on some charge or other made by the Band Sergeant (I don't remember exactly what.) For reasons unknown, the Company Commander remanded me for CO's Orders. In due course I appeared before the Commanding Officer which meant I had to have my uniform in tip top order which, of course, took time. The punishment I received (seven days confined to barracks) was minimal but would be entered on my Army Form 121, which meant it would take two years good conduct to remove, whereby if the Company Commander had awarded the same it would have been entered on my Army Form 120 and taken only one year to remove.

As a defaulter, I had to report to the guard room whenever the call was sounded. This usually ran in a fairly organised fashion except at week ends when everyone else was off-duty and the guard commander was in a bad mood because he had drawn the short straw.

The normal routine started half an hour after reveille when you paraded, washed and shaved in working dress of the day. This early parade had a good side in that after dismiss you could go to the dining room and obtain a mug of tea before the usual morning rush. You then went about your daily tasks until 17:30hrs, when you paraded in fatigues to be directed to some task or other around the camp area. This could range from cook house fatigues – spud bashing, washing down the working or dining areas – to cleaning out the storm drains or generally smartening up the camp. I always had the feeling it depended upon where the CO had been 'visiting' that day. Around 19:30 you were allowed a break, which meant you were allowed to visit the canteen to partake of refreshment, though it was a foolish man who turned out for the next parade smelling of drink. The next call was at 20:00 hrs, when you paraded with an item of kit specified by the guard commander.

Defaulters call was sounded every half hour, which meant you were dashing backwards and forwards with short periods in between to prepare your kit. If you were lucky a friend, possibly out of boredom, would help, in that he would prepare some item or other. At 22:00 hrs the *Last Post* would be sounded and the orderly officer of the day would be on parade to inspect the defaulters. The dress would be starched and pressed jungle trousers, flannel shirt, belt, gaiters and best beret in place of your hat jungle. Whether or not you had an easy inspection depended very much upon the mood of the orderly officer who might be on a punishment duty himself, in which case he could be a little sympathetic. Or he could be on the normal rota, in which case he did not want to be there himself so why worry about these offenders in front of him?

One of the problems was the condition of the ground. Your boots were always either dusty or covered in mud. There was little one could do except get a little crafty. I knew one of the store-men of Head Quarter Company Stores, which were situated not only near the guard room, but also near the tarmac road which ran past the guard room. I would take my best boots and cleaning kit to my friend's bunk, either during the lunch break or during the evening canteen break, so was able to get changed between the last two calls, thus able to present myself fairly clean. With regards to orderly officers, I have seen men told to remove their boots to see if they had any holes in their socks. Once I was told to dismantle my belt and remove my cap badge to see if they had been cleaned front and back Having been a Boy, I was in the habit of cleaning most brasses back and front so was able to show a clean set. My cap badge shank was stamped with my number This raised some comment from the officer but at least I got through.

While on the subject of orderly officers and guard duty, I should relate an incident that still raises a laugh at reunions.

The battalion was out on manoeuvres and the band had to provide a guard over a section of the camp. Our 'arms' were entrenching tool handles. The Officer concerned was fresh from Sandhurst and full of book learning and methods. After inspecting the so-called guard and immediate area, he addressed one of the bandsmen. 'If you came under fire and had to take cover in that fox hole, what would be your field of fire?'

The bandsman replied without a moment's hesitation. 'As far as I could throw this f——g entrenching tool handle, Sir!'

I thought the officer would blow his lid, but he took a deep breath and dismissed us. I think he learned something that night.

The Army Kinema Corporation had a cinema erected on the camp as soon as a 'reliable' generator was made available and in use. The outside walls were of hessian, supported by very long angle irons. Although this material allowed the sound through, the picture was very distorted so there was no point at all in standing outside! The seating was made from shaped bamboo in which the small buttons of your great coat got caught and torn off when you stood up. Many a morning you would see NCOs and men searching the ground beneath the seats in an attempt to retrieve these small buttons. This may seem strange, but as the buttons were of regimental design they were hard to come by and it was imperative they were recovered if possible. You may wonder why we wore our great-coats at all in the tropics, but the evenings could be chilly, especially in the open.

On occasion when we were queuing for admission to the cinema some of the men used to try to catch glow worms and place them in a jar to see if they would provide a light of some sort! It was pretty daft idea, but it kept them amused.

The generator that powered the projector also provided

lighting in all the tents which previously had been provided by hurricane lamps, or Tilley lamps, a better class of hurricane lamp the majority of which the tent occupants had brought for themselves. Paraffin was made available through the company stores We quickly learned to maintain these lamps in good order as the generator had a habit of breaking down. When this occurred there would be a great shout from all over the camp plus some very uncomplimentary advice for the Engineers. In fact, the large number of switch-offs almost made it a way of life.

One morning I was greeted by a bandsman, pointing towards the area where the Governor's parade had been held. 'What are this lot up to?' he asked.

I looked across to see a party of men dressed in the casual way of the RAF, carrying theodolites, metal surveyors' tapes and large chart boards. They appeared to measure over a large area. When they departed we thought little more of it until one morning a very large convoy appeared and started to unload all manner of tools, massive metal pins plus very large rolls of what appeared to be tarpaulin. We couldn't stay and watch as we had our own duties to perform but when we returned at lunchtime we saw what they were about.

The tarpaulins had been laid and pinned down to form a fairly smooth surface to enable aircraft to land and take off. At least, that's what we and, possibly, they thought.

The time came when the first aircraft – a group of Spitfires – attempted to land. The whole camp stood around watching and waiting.

The first Spitfire made a very low pass over the 'runway' before climbing away to come round to land. It came in and touched down, having made a good job of his approach, but his prop wash got under the tarpaulin and lifted it up in to the path of the next plane, which had been circling overhead waiting instruction to land. The ground crews dashed about getting the landing surface in order. In came the second Spitfire and made a good landing, but with the same effect on the tarpaulin.

Having got the two aircraft down, they had to attempt getting them airborne again. The take-off had the same effect upon the tarpaulins, and it was now obvious they would have to work out a solution.

The RAF departed and nothing was seen for some time until one morning we heard vehicles moving about and the sound of metal being dropped onto the ground. Upon investigation it was apparent that the RAF personnel had returned, bringing with them a large number of perforated steel planks, similar to those we'd seen on the newsreels during the war being laid to provide landing strips all over the world.

I wondered why they hadn't brought these planks in the first place. Maybe it was too simple an idea. In any event, it worked, and we soon got so used to the sound of aircraft taking off and landing that we took no notice of them at all.

The emergency in Malaya was becoming more serious and the original 29th Brigade was dispatched there. This meant not only the loss of the Cameronians, the Wiltshire Regiment and the Ghurka Rifles but also meant an increase in the role of the remaining regiments, as well as more work for the military and dance bands.

Before the departure of the Ghurkas, we were given the opportunity to purchase a Kukri – their fighting knives – suitably engraved with our number, regiment and date. The one I bought now hangs on the wall in my mother-in-law's house.

With a view to the possible role of the regiment in the future, an officer who had served in Burma gave us a series of talks on the use of bamboo – not just as something to hang your coat on or from which to hang your mosquito net but as a source of clean drinking water, also as a cooking utensil in which to cook your rice. As things turned out we never had the opportunity to put his advice into practice.

One evening some of the band decided to go into the local village and take in a film showing at the cinema there. About half way through the main feature there was an explosion, as we learned later, in the gentlemen's toilet. The Chinese in the audience became very excited, leapt to their feet and beat a very noisy retreat. I must admit to feeling a little disturbed but as we were in the balcony we showed our British Grit (or stupidity) and remained in our seats. The only sign of any disturbance among us was when one of our number asked me if I had a cigarette.

'You don't smoke,' I said.

'I do now!' he grunted.

I know the line's been used in many movies, but it really happened that night.

After a time the Chinese started to come back into the cinema but were making an infernal din. Suddenly a British voice shouted, 'Shut up!'

This only had the effect of starting the Chinese off again! We eventually saw the picture but never found out the cause of the explosion.

Whenever we travelled through any of the villages, we would hear a boy clacking together a percussion instrument consisting of two pieces of hard wood as he walked through the streets. The dance band needed that effect to use in their Latin American numbers and managed to secure some, but we never found out why the boys patrolled the streets as they did.

About this time I gave some thought to the matter of promotion and realised that to climb onto the lowest rung of the ladder you required your Army Certificate of Education, 3rd Class. I admit I felt a little apprehensive but found I had little to worry about as the subjects and syllabus were much the same as I'd been taught at school. The only addition was a comprehension test.

I was given a card upon which was printed a passage from some book or other. Having read the card, I left the hut and made my way to a tent which had been pitched some way off, in which resided an officer who would ask questions about the passage I'd just read.

I'm glad to say I got my certificate!

The toilet arrangements were of the 'thunder box' variety, which were emptied daily and we often wondered where the contents were taken, until one of the of the colour sergeants found out. The NCO concerned was travelling through a village on the way to Kowloon and had been giving the driver advice on how to keep his 15cwt truck a safe distance from the road edge. Exactly what happened we never did find out but the result was that the truck ploughed into a stack of 'night soil' buckets piled on the road side to await collection by a farmer for use on his rice paddies. (Despite this, I still like a rice pudding!)

15cwt trucks at this time had split windscreens consisting of two pieces of glass 15"x15" with a large gap between the panes, so there was practically no way to prevent the "night soil" from squelching into the cab. The driver got an awful ribbing when he got back to the camp, while the Sergeants' Mess had a field day!

Christmas Day was celebrated in the usual way when the Army is abroad. There was no reveille, and the day started with the Platoon Officers and NCOs waking the men with mugs of 'Gun fire' (This was a very strong brew of tea, heavily laced with rum and is a custom carried only by regiments which had seen service in India, therefore unknown in the Brigade of Guards.) It was time then for leg-pulling and fun-making but I remembered the RSM's words from the year before. 'Today is your day; the other three hundred and sixty four are mine!' And some NCOs and officers had long memories.

As always the day would be filled with all sorts of activities, the first of which would be a short church service at which the band would play carols and festive music, followed by a Sergeants' Mess versus Officers' Mess football match, which bore no resemblance to any match played under FA rules!

The number of players on each side was of little consequence, as long as they were in fancy dress. The match, once started, could go on for an undetermined time, usually until both teams took a break for a drink, which also became a contest!

The band usually provided popular light music in the dining hall during the Christmas lunch period. On this particular day, the Pioneers had built a stage upon which we set up. One of the band was unable to finish the programme. It is the only time I have seen a man slide over the edge of a platform and disappear underneath it! We took little notice of him as we still had a programme to finish and we couldn't have our lunch until we did. It wasn't until early evening that we remembered the chap's debacle, and then only when some one asked if we had seen him. Upon investigation we discovered that he was still under the stage, fast asleep in the foetal position, with his instrument clutched to him, completely unaware he had missed the greater part of the day's festivities.

Shortly after Christmas, the tents of Head Quarter Company had to be moved to a position about hundred yards from where they were. We were not sure why until a large number of workers, male and female, employed by a contractor, arrived. I have never ceased to be amazed at the loads the Hakar women carried on bamboo poles across their shoulders. There seemed to be no strict rules about this, other than, 'If I can lift it, I can carry it'! The Hakar women were distinctive in their head-dress, which was very stiff, at least 2' across with a hole in the middle perched on the centre of their heads and with a 9" pelmet of pleated black material.

Just after we moved and before we had time to dig drainage ditches, the heavens opened and everywhere was flooded. It took some time to get things dry and back in a reasonable order again.

It turned out that in these conditions, the most useful item issued in our tropical kit was the poncho. The poncho not only covered one in a much better fashion than the old ground sheet, but was made in such a way as to allow the wearer to tighten a draw string around the neck thereby closing the material and making it completely waterproof. When clipped together with another poncho it made a fairly comfortable field tent. (Not that we ever had to use it that way.)

The other piece of tropical equipment that proved very popular with us was *hat, jungle, green*. This was issued in place of *hat, bush*, which had proved not only expensive but very cumbersome under jungle conditions. The *hat, jungle, green* proved very versatile and it was amazing the different styles that came about. We wore ours with a flat brim while the South Staffs wore theirs with the left hand of the brim turned up and held in place with their regimental badge.

Inevitably, before much time had elapsed, they were subject to a new instruction. 'Men will keep their hats clean.'

This led to the practice of men scrubbing their hats then stretching them over a steel helmet and leaving them in the sun to dry. Very soon the hats changed from jungle green to almost white. As the jungle hat was never worn outside camp unless on duty, it meant we still had to keep our berets up to standard.

When the better weather arrived, the contractor's work started to take shape. It appeared they were building permanent barrack blocks and speculation ran riot!

Were we to be the lucky ones?

Were the RAF moving in?

A SHROPSHIRE BOY

In the end the powers that be decided the *all* the Infantry battalions were to be camped near to the border, and the Royal Tank Regiment would be the new occupiers of Sek Kong.

Around this time a major who was one of the company commanders died, and a full military funeral was required. This meant that the band and bugles were on duty, plus an officer bearer party and an escort from his company, as befitted his rank.

During rehearsal it came to light that the boy playing the cymbals was not too certain about where to clash them in one of the funeral marches. The bass drummer came up with the idea that as the clash came in a part where the bass drum was of less importance, if the boy held out the cymbal towards him, he would give it a whack. All went well in rehearsal and the matter was settled, or so we thought.

On the day of the parade to the cemetery, the first couple of clashes went to plan, but either the boy moved towards the drummer or the drummer moved, because all that was heard was a dull thwack and a loud 'F——g Hell!'

I think the colonel who was marching behind must have been in a benevolent mood because he came over after the parade was ended to ask if the boy was alright, which of course he was, apart from a rather bruised hand.

As the Military Cemetery is situated across the road from the Happy Valley, either the man who planned the racecourse or the man who planned the cemetery must have had quite a sense of humour to have placed the last resting place across the road from the winning post!

The band also played at the racecourse on a fairly regular basis and always set up in the Silver Stand area against the track fence but facing the members' grandstand. Nothing wrong with that, you might say, but as the Chinese ladies had the habit of sitting with their feet resting up on the bars of the rails and as they were wearing chocksons, there were quite a few wrong notes played on those days. We were young men; who could blame us?

The Band and Bugles were issued with No 3 Dress uniforms, which were much cooler than Jungle Greens, also smarter, even if they did require a lot more attention. The buttons were of the type that were held in place by a split ring inserted into a loop on the back of the button which had been passed through a sewn hole in the jacket. This manoeuvre had to be gone through every time you handed in, or received the uniform back from the laundry. You also had to remove the band 'Harp' and, in the case of NCOs, their chevrons. Most of us kept these removable items in an empty Woodbine cigarette tin which originally held 50 Export cigarettes. We also transported the uniform in a wicker case which cost around one dollar (when the HK$ was worth about 7½p). When the uniforms came back from the Chinese contractor, who, if required would wash and press them in 48 hours, there was always one problem. The uniforms were very heavily starched and you had literally to tear them apart to get into them! We were also issued with two pairs of shorts of a pattern as worn by the Ghurkas. These shorts were much wider in the leg and had a wider waist band. In fact they were altogether much smarter and definitely more comfortable, but they were kept for ceremonial occasions only.

It was decided that it would be a good public relations exercise if the Massed Bands together with the Massed Pipes and Drums and Buglers of the Division gave a display of music and marching in Kowloon. I remember what a colourful array the Ghurkha wives in their saris made when seated in the stands.

After the rehearsal the senior bandmaster called all the performers together and informed them: 'In the event of inclement weather – that's pissing down to you ignorant lot – ponchos will be worn and the programme shortened to platform performance only. Let's hope for the best.'

IT DID NOT RAIN!

The musical performance contained the overture *Finlandia* conducted by the bandmaster of the Argyll and Sutherland Highlanders with much kilt swinging but although the rostrum was raised I think the audience was just too far away to appreciate this. The performance, like most military programmes, finished off with the *1812 Overture*, with plenty of bangs and crashes, in this case provided by twenty-five-pounder field guns situated behind the platform. During rehearsal the guns had not been fired and we'd relied on the trigger mechanism just clicking. Come the performance, they scared the daylights out of the population and dislodged some of the planks of the platform with the result some music stands had to be grabbed fairly quickly. However, all ended to everyone's satisfaction and I felt we had done a good job, even if the locals may not have agreed.

As had been rumoured, our move to another area took place so we were destined not to see the completion of the new barracks. The camp we were to occupy turned out to be hutted accommodation which, although inclined to be hotter than living under canvas, had the advantage of being dry during the rainy season. The new area was named San Wai and was situated about a mile from the railway station where the line crossed the river which formed the border between the New Territories and 'Red' China at Fan Ling. This was very handy following a night out in Kowloon as you could catch a train at Kowloon station which departed at midnight and arrived in Fan Ling approximately three quarters of an hour later. This of course meant a walk back to camp but this sobering walk certainly kept some out of the clutches of the Regimental Police.

I believe the camp had been built some years before our occupation as in the hill behind it were two very large regimental badges, made of white pebbles, of regiments who had obviously been stationed here in past years. (Not so long ago I got into conversation with an ex-soldier who had been amongst the last regiments to serve in this area and he assured me that they were still there at that time, but no doubt the Chinese authorities would now have their own ideas about these badges!)

The ablutions were quite different than those in Sek Kong, in that they had white porcelain hand basins and proper shower stalls. The toilet furniture consisted of a concrete square with a hole in the centre and a foot pad either side of the hole. It took some time to get used to squatting instead of sitting.

As was the norm when the battalion went into the hills on exercise, the band and odd bods were left to work and guard the camp. On one occasion I was set to painting the outside of the guard room.

The floor of the guard room was concrete, while the walls both inner and outer were of corrugated iron sheets, fixed to a wooden frame. The bars of the cells were set top and bottom into wooden lintels 8" x 8", which were bolted top and bottom into the frame of the construction. I was merrily painting away when I was addressed by a voice from inside.

'Don't press too hard on the bars.'

'Why not?' I asked.

'Step back and I'll show you.'

I stepped back and the chap inside tapped on one side of the bar frame and the whole bar block swung out on its bolts. He told me that in the night he would climb out and go for a stroll. I still wonder if he carried on with these midnight flits after the battalion got back. As the saying goes, 'Who dares wins!'

The RSM always addressed new drafts sent to the battalion for three reasons:

[1] To introduce himself to the new arrivals.

[2] To see what the Depot had sent out to us.

[3] To give them some advice on the life in Hong Kong.

The main theme of the latter was to advise them regarding what these days is called Social Disease, and to drill home the use of preventative stations around the towns and the penalties for not using them after sex with 'one of the ladies'. The RSM had just finished talking to the draft when there came a voice from the ranks.

'I don't go with women, Sir.'

The RSM kept very calm and facing the lad answered *sotto voce*. 'Out here, even the angels can get it!'

As a result of this exchange the recruit obtained the nick name 'Angel', which stuck with him throughout his service with the battalion.

While talking of matters sexual, there was a recurring incident to which I could never quite find a reasonable solution. Our beds were of the double bunk variety and I was fortunate, or unfortunate, to get a top bunk not only near the door but also adjacent to one of the roof fans which were kept rotating all hours of the day or night. 'Lucky,' I hear you say, but it wasn't so.

The lower bunk was occupied by a bandsman who masturbated every night! The bunk fittings were rather loose and the whole assembly rocked. I was able to prevent this going on too long by releasing his mosquito net which was wedged under my mattress. I never heard one word of protest and, to this day, I'm sure he thought the net had descended through his actions. (I wonder if he will read this and finally learn the truth?)

It was while in San Wai I learnt what was meant by a 'School' in the old India service. Some of the old India men would get together, drink their pay away, then borrow up to the limit of their next pay. Each man in the school borrowed in turn so that they had drink every night. This suited people like myself who wanted to save a few dollars but would have otherwise spent it. The school *always* paid their debts on pay day, and would carry on in this fashion until the day they all decided to go dry. They would pay off their debts and stay sober – miserable but sober – until the next 'term' started.

At this time we all received a Local Overseas Allowance. If you were able to ignore this LOA, you could build a healthy credit balance, thus enabling you to have good civilian clothes made to measure, which meant you could enjoy the night life of both Kowloon and Hong Kong. Minor problems did arise in that a large number of squaddies seemed to have a preference for camel hair jackets and chocolate trousers while others chose very colourful shirts and dark trousers. The biggest problem was that you could always tell a serviceman by his hair cut – short back and sides and plenty on top! No matter what you tried, it always came back to, 'What's under your hat is yours but the rest belongs to the Army!'. However, we did get away from this for a time when the battalion left us in Kowloon.

The dance band as always was very busy. On one occasion they were approached by a chap who was obviously a serviceman who asked if they minded if he sang with them. The Band Sergeant agreed, and gave him a chance. It turned out that the man had a good voice and style. Later he turned professional under the name of Matt Monro

One venue the dance band often played was the Fleet Club on Hong Kong Island, as a result of which the band was able to arrange to use the facilities of the club for changing whenever they had an engagement in Hong Kong and not have too much worry about the journey down from San Wai. The whole band could spend any local leave at the club if they wished and enjoy the facilities. Not every member of the band spent his leave this way, in fact one made his way to Macau and, from what we heard, had a wonderful time. On more than one occasion I stayed in camp to act as storeman and postman, which meant I was able to enjoy a certain freedom, and get into Hong Kong every other day.

To reach Hong Kong proper you had to board one of the White Star ferries, either vehicular or foot passenger. I believe this journey today is via the new tunnel, but then there was another alternative. These were small boats 'manned' by women, but you used these only as a very last resort or in an emergency as these women had quite a dodgy reputation. They were said usually to be connected with the prostitute or drugs trade.

Inevitably a couple of interesting incidents occurred on the ferries. The first was connected with the bugler who'd been so ill aboard *The Empress of Australia*. The poor chap couldn't even cross the harbour without being really sick. He tried everything from travel sickness pills just before he left camp to various home-made remedies, but nothing seemed to work. The amazing thing was that directly he stepped off the ferry he was as right as rain, and could carry out his duty as though nothing had happened.

The other incident occurred one night after performing in Hong Kong. The band were aboard a 3-ton lorry on the vehicular ferry, parked behind a civilian car carrying a European family consisting, as we found out, of father, mother, young son and younger daughter. Soldiers being soldiers attracted the children's attention by pulling faces and generally acting the fool. Eventually father got out and came back to our transport, and we thought we were in for a right ear-wigging, but to our amazement he invited us all back to their apartment for something to eat and drink. We accepted, of course, but had some doubts about the truck driver, as he might want to get back. Our fears were unfounded as it turned out the driver was on 'defaulters', and was doing this duty as part of his punishment so was in no hurry at all.

We followed their car back to their home and were treated

right royally. As we were leaving, our host took another bandsman and myself to one side and informed us that we were welcome to come to the family home any time we were free. Needless to say we accepted his offer and made many visits to him and his family up to the time his work took him to Australia. It turned out that he worked for an import/export merchant who was a millionaire. When I first met his employer I found it difficult to get my mind around the fact that he was so rich. He wore old, baggy grey flannel trousers and a sports coat with leather patches on the elbows and many cigarette burns. I once asked him why he dressed in this fashion when he was so rich, to which he replied. 'Some people have to dress to appear that they look like millionaires. I don't have to because I am one!'

One evening our new found friend told us his boss was setting up a branch of his company in Australia and he was going to run the new set up. Would we like a job with him?

We thought hard and long about this, especially as it would mean being away from our families even longer. In fact we were on the verge of accepting his offer when the Korean War broke out and all discharges by purchase were stopped.

As far as military duties were concerned we carried on as usual –Governor's Guard mounts and dismounts, Guards of Honour for such persons as the new General Officer Commanding (General Mansergh). We also carried on with concerts in public venues, one of which was the Tiger Balm Gardens. The Tiger Balm Gardens were situated high up on the Peak and had been created by a Chinese businessman who had made his fortune from an ointment which was sold in very small circular metal containers. The gardens, like the ointment, were very effective and soothed away many a headache.

The band also made quite a number of broadcasts and recordings for the British Forces Network. Public relations raised their head again and it was decided to repeat the Massed Bands Pipes and Drums 'Spectacular', only this time on Hong Kong proper. Our billet for this period was a barracks overlooking Stanley Township. When we took over the billet, the problem was that all the windows, frames and all, had been removed and, as the barracks directly faced the sea, from which there a keen wind blew most of the time, it wasn't the ideal place to hang one's hat! I managed to acquire a very large piece of heavy canvas with which I blocked off the seaward end of my lower bunk so at least was able to get some sleep without feeling too cold.

The rehearsals took place in a chill, biting wind and as we were wearing tropical jungle greens, none of us were too happy! Of course, we took precautions against feeling too cold during the actual performances. No one in the audience could have realised that underneath my No 3 Dress I was wearing a thick vest, long johns plus pyjamas. I wonder how our Scottish friends got on. It must have been uncomfortable, to say the least.

Another engagement (paid) was the Far East premiere of the film *They Were Not Divided*. This was held in a cinema in the HK District of Wanchai. I wondered why this district was chosen as it had a fairly dodgy reputation, owing to the large number of 'ladies' who plied their trade in the streets and houses nearby. The band arrived early so as to set up on stage before the invited audience arrived. After setting up we had to wait behind the silver screen. It was here I learned something that has fascinated me ever since. The screen was made up of hundreds and hundreds of small marbles like glass balls. How this worked, I have yet to discover.

The time for our performance came just as the cinema manager was telling us how to get to our reserved seats in the rear of the dress circle. Some of the band missed the greater part of his directions, and therefore had difficulty in finding their places. We entertained the audience for some time before we received the signal that the Governor had arrived in the auditorium. We played the national anthem, removed our gear then went off to find our seats via rear passages and corridors. I knew of at least two who didn't make it. When the performance was over, we made our way in the reverse direction or, at least, so we thought, to collect our instruments but very few of the band made it at the first attempt. Asking a Chinese attendant whose English seemed to extend no further than 'Ticket, please,' made some rather late.

In August 1950, as the Hong Kong garrison were the nearest British troops to Korea it was decided that two infantry battalions would move to support the Americans, although, by this time, the United Nations were beginning to join in a combined effort. The two battalions chosen were the Middlesex Regiment and the Argyll and Sutherland Highlanders. The two battalions with a shortfall in manpower being made up from the regiments remaining behind. The KSLI provided quite a number. In view of what was happening, training was stepped up, while once again, the band and Odds & Sods were left to keep guard over the camp.

The Chinese farmers carried out a 'burn off' at times so as to provide nitrates for their fields. They would leave the natural fertiliser on the ground and hope it would rain. The only problem from our point of view was that the burning could sneak under the barbed wire fence, possibly endangering our huts and equipment. However there seemed to be no communication problem, despite the lack of a common tongue. Just the tone of one's 'request' seemed to do the trick!

On one occasion I was patrolling with my trusty entrenching tool handle when I saw a movement in the dark in an area where the barbed wire passed over a dip in the ground. I stood back in the shadow of a hut, got the sinking feeling in my stomach under control and lowered myself into a crouch position and watched the 'shape' attempting to ease itself under the wire. Luckily for me, it got snagged on the barbs. I chose this moment to issue the time worn challenge: 'Halt! Who goes there?'

There was no response from the 'shape'. I repeated the challenge twice more, but still with no response. I issued the challenge once again, adding rather desperately, 'Or I fire!'

This time there was a response from the figure.

'Stop f—ing about and get me off this f—ing wire!'

It turned out to be one of the lads who had been down to the village and had lost his intoxicated way in the dark. We both had a good laugh, especially the lad when he found out I was armed with nothing more deadly than an entrenching tool handle.

Christmas came round again and after the morning 'Gun fire' and the obligatory football matches, we were free. Someone discovered that if you got hold of a piece of down-pipe, jammed one end in the ground, dropped a couple of Chinese fire-crackers in the open end, then closed it with an empty cigarette tin, it made a very effective 'mortar', with the tin travelling a considerable distance. Before long there were quite a few mock battles going on between various platoons. Angel tried to liven things up by tying rockets to the various telephone and electric cables strung around the camp. The only thing wrong with this idea was that once you had attached, lit and released the rocket, you had no control over it. In fact quite a number ended in the bunks of WOs and Sergeants, although by this time most of these were well under the influence and beyond caring. They didn't realise until later what damage had been done to their quarters. The sounds of our battles were so realistic that the South Staffs across the valley alerted their Internal Security Platoon and sent someone across to assess the situation! (The Internal Security Platoon was an instant readiness platoon provided by each battalion in turn to go to the aid of the civil power if required during a time of civil unrest, as in Northern Ireland.)

I found it very strange that although the two battalions were camped opposite each other on either side of the valley, they never seemed to mix especially as they came from neighbouring counties. Maybe that was the trouble, although the 'Heavies' and the Light Infantry never became too friendly either. I never did discover why that was. Maybe the Light and Brights were just so much better?

It came about that the sport of competitive bayonet fencing was to be revived and as far as our part of the world was concerned, the finals would be held in Singapore. The idea of a trip to Singapore was much to my liking so I volunteered. The contestants wore face masks, rather like those used for sword fencing, but much heavier, with very thick leather sides.

One 'fought' with a dummy rifle with a plunger instead of a bayonet, which nevertheless weighed about the same as a normal rifle. The fencer wore a very heavily padded jacket much akin to those used to restrain violent persons, also a thick padded glove on the hand towards your opponent, with a lighter glove on the other hand. You were allowed to defend yourself even if your rifle was knocked from your leading hand, in which case you used the butt.

I did fairly well until, during a really rough bout, I received a blow to the side of my mask which despite the thickness of the leather made my ears ring and sting for days. I decided then that the trip to Singapore just wasn't worth the pain!

CHAPTER SIX

Soldiers, into battle go. (anon)

April 25th 1951 saw the battalion boarding the *USS Montrose* to be transported to Korea to relieve the Middlesex Regiment. Naturally we were there to play them away, but while we waited for them to leave I heard an announcement over the ship's Tannoy.

'There are now twenty two players on the ball team!'

It puzzled me for years until I happened to mention it at a reunion a couple of years ago. Apparently, this was just the captain's way of telling the crew that another of their number had contracted a 'social disease. A novel euphemism, to say the least.

After cleaning up the camp in preparation for the next set of occupants, who were likely to be one of the battalions returning from Korea, the band were posted to be attached to the 40th Division Battle School where a large number of the battalion's kit bags were in store. It became the band's responsibility to read any casualty lists and search through the hundreds of kit bags for any belonging to the names appearing. The named kit having been found it would then be searched for items such as 'saucy' photographs or books that might be offensive to relatives back home. Having got through the search, the kit would then be dispatched to Blighty.

Fortunately we didn't have to carry out this duty very often, but a problem arose when the band were posted away and the stores were left in the care of the Battle School staff. Quite a number of the battalion had kit stolen or, at least, damaged and some still 'call the band', even to this day, without knowing what really happened or why.

The 40th Division Battle School was a hutted camp situated on a road in Kowloon, with a main road running in front of the gates and railway track passing behind. It always seemed a strange place to locate a Battle School although we didn't wonder out loud as we were able to walk into town instead of taking the white-knuckle-ride of the cliff road between San Wai and Kowloon. This road literally clung to the cliff face but was just wide enough to allow vehicles to pass in either direction at the same time. Owing to the severity of the bends and drops, the Military Police used to put up huge signs: 'It's a long drop if you can't stop!' or, 'A 15cwt truck went over here last week!'

I openly admit that whenever I travelled the road, I smoked far more than normal, although I doubt if this helped in any way.

The Battle School was manned by personnel whose parent units would hardly miss them and whose absence would certainly not be a drain on their strength! Some of the staff seemed to be complete strangers to discipline, despite the best efforts of the camp warrant officer (a battery sergeant-major of the Royal Artillery). This BSM sported a magnificent moustache, at least twelve inches each side! It was rumoured that he slept with his head between two wooden blocks to prevent him turning over in the night, but as there was no visible confirmation of this while we were in the camp, it must remain a rumour.

On the camp lived and worked a Chinese contractor who, for some unknown reason, would not let me have my weekly laundry until I had recited my regimental number in his native tongue, i.e.: Chinese! (Say Ling Say Yee Bat Sam Ling). Maybe he thought it might come in handy if I were ever taken prisoner by his fellow countrymen.

We still had Band Boys with us and one day one of them turned up with a monkey which he wanted to keep as a pet in his hut. Nobody thought this a good idea, but as things turned out it didn' remain an issue for very long. The monkey either didn't like the diet the boy fed it, or it just gave up the will to live, to meet a fiery end in the camp's incinerator, which heated the water for showers and washing up.

One day a huge parade was held in Kowloon but, as we were detached, we were not concerned, except as spectators from various bars along the route. It started to rain. This wasn't unheard of and shouldn't have been a problem, but the ladies of the Hong Kong Naval Reserve were dressed in white uniforms, and we all know what happens to white cotton material when it gets wet. It becomes almost transparent. The rain hammered down even harder as they marched on, with the result that there were almost naked ladies on parade.

It beggars belief how fast some people can move from one place to another! The British service personnel I felt sorry for were the Pipes and Drums of the Argyll and Sutherland Highlanders, just returned from Korea, therefore looked on as heroes, who had to carry on regardless, whatever the weather, and stick with it! Drum skins in those days were still made of animal skins and when wet were not only prone to stretch but also to split, therefore, unlike today's plastic 'skins', they had to be treated rather gently under such circumstances.

It was inevitable that sooner or later I needed of some dental treatment and was taken to a Mobile Dental Surgery situated on a hillside slope above the town of Tai Po in the New Territories. I'll never understand why I wasn't taken to the 33rd General Hospital which was situated in the Kowloon suburbs, just up the road from the Battle School, but that's the army.

The surgery was open to the elements but as I remember it was a pleasant, sunny day so that didn't matter. There was no electricity supply at the time of my visit, which meant the drill was operated by a foot pedal. The dentist, a captain from the Royal Army Dental Corps, liked to talk and the more he talked the more it took his attention away from the task in hand – or should I say foot? The more he talked, the slower the drill rotation, and I spent a nasty long time in the chair, resulting in a very aching set of teeth. I doubt if I'll ever forget the red-headed captain and his foot-powered drill.

One day there appeared in the camp a group of soldiers wearing *Feld Grau*, and leather gaiters, such as worn by gamekeepers. Upon investigation it was discovered they were Portugese Infantry, stationed at Macau, who because of the close ties between Britain and Portugal, had been sent to Hong Kong and taken on the strength of the Battle School to be taught our platoon and company tactics. At least that's what we were told, but judging by their evening manoeuvres, I feel it was an opportunity for Rest & Recuperation, not to be missed! The soldiers concerned were, except for the NCOs, all conscripts and we were amazed to learn that they had to hire their rifles from the Army. We wondered how this would go down in the British services. Although they were poorly paid there was a large Portugese civilian population in Hong Kong who rallied round so there was little they lacked during their stay in the colony.

Just along the road from the camp was a very good NAAFI club from which many of the broadcasts were made by the British Forces Network. The band took part in various light entertainment shows in the club's lounge. These were held about once a fortnight with nearly everyone involved being service personnel One taking part on a fairly regular basis was a corporal from the Royal Military Police who, after telling various stories and jokes, always finished his act with, 'Taking your time from the village clock,' then, beating time with two mess tins (closed) on his thigh, would belt out some rendition or other. I suppose someone must have loved him.

The hairdressers in the club were absolutely brilliant! Every Friday after pay parade we would make our way to the club to enjoy the luxury of hot facial towels, a decent hair cut and a little pampering, followed by a very good meal. The staff in the club were equally as good as those employed in the *Peninsular Hotel* opposite. (The *Peninsular* was the one chosen to accommodate the crews of aircraft during their wait over, pending the next leg of their journey to Australia or Japan. This was in the days before jet travel, when some air journeys took several days.

One rather amusing incident took place in the bar of the *Peninsular*. A soda siphon had been placed in the ice bucket on the counter without any one noticing that it was in the path of sunlight streaming in through a bottle-bottom pane of glass.

A SHROPSHIRE BOY

After a short space of time there was an almighty bang and many present were showered with glass and ice cubes. A passing member of the Hong Kong Police dashed in, with revolver drawn, took a quick look around and withdrew leaving those present to sort themselves out. (I bet he made an entry in his pocket book.)

After everyone had picked themselves up either from the floor or from behind articles of padded furniture, we all had a good laugh and got back to the serious business, drinking!

The dance band had become friendly with a group of Filipino musicians through many engagements they'd carried out together. One Sunday they invited them into the camp for a session. The dining room provided just the right space and acoustics. They made a wonderful sound which had to be heard to be believed and I doubt if such a session could ever be brought together again.

After some time a member of the camp staff, who had the misfortune to be on gate duty, plus two European members of the HK Police came into the dining room and informed the performers that their sound was being enjoyed so much by the local population that there was a slight problem in keeping the area outside 'safe' for pedestrians. Although they didn't want to be seen as killjoys, they asked if the band would close the doors and windows.

It was not long after this we were told we were joining the battalion in, Korea – not as stretcher-bearers but *as a band*! We would shortly be boarding a Royal Navy vessel to be transported to Japan

A P Sisley

CHAPTER SEVEN

Set every threadbare sail. (Holmes)

August 4th 1951 saw us loading our stores onto a naval barge, into which we all then climbed to be transported into mid harbour, where the aircraft-carrier *HMS Warrior* was swinging on her cable, waiting to carry us on the first stage of our next journey. *HMS Warrior* had been de-mothballed from the reserve fleet and was manned, in the main, by reservists, of whom many were not in the best of moods at being called back into the service.

We came alongside and ascended a gangway, at the top of which stood a rather robust Chief Petty Officer and the Officer of the Watch. One or two members of the band had been in the Sea Cadets and knew the drill about saluting the Quarter deck, but most of us were ignorant of such matters. In the main we were ignorant pongos, according to the Petty Officer who every so often was heard to mutter, in mild disgust, 'Pongos on ships! They'll be putting doors on the heads next!' (For those not familiar with the jargon, 'heads' is the naval term for toilets. I have my own idea of why there were no doors on the toilets but I will leave the reader to their own reasoning.)

Having found our way to the hanger deck to help load our stores on board through a cargo door in the ship's side, we went to our designated mess (No 306 Mess). Unlike our journey on the *Empress of Australia*, we had no hammocks, so bedded down on lockers, table-tops or the floor. It seems that every *matelot* had his own hammock which was part of his personal kit that he took from ship to ship, so hard luck, pongos!

The *Warrior* set sail later that day but not before we had heard a series of controlled gun shots. We enquired the nature of this event and were told it was to honour Her Majesty, Queen Elizabeth's Birthday. I suddenly remembered that the next day, (the 5th) was my 21st, but decided to keep shtum, as I knew what the others could get up to. However, I think someone must have known, as I was rostered to be mess orderly for the day.

I arose as usual, washed, and was half way through shaving when a 'pipe' gave the command, 'Cooks to the galley'.

I turned to a sailor next to me. 'Breakfast is going to be late this morning.'

'What do you mean?' he asked.

'They've only just called the cooks to the galley.'

'You berk!' the sailor said. 'That means that the representative of the mess has to collect the meal from the galley!'

I wiped myself off and made my way as quickly as I could via the mess deck to the galley. I was about to learn that corridors and passageways on warships are not built straight and certainly not on one level. I eventually found the galley and fell somewhat breathlessly through the hatch to be greeted by the bulky frame of the Chief Petty Officer in charge, standing with arms akimbo and a nasty look on his face. 'Where the hell have you been until now?'

I told him I was sorry but I hadn't yet got used to the ship's lay out. The CPO softened a little and allowed one of the cooks to give me the mess breakfast. As the Chief turned away I heard words that were to ring in my ears for days: 'Pongos on ships!'

Life on board was fairly relaxed for, as we soon discovered, the flight deck was twisted from midships to the bow and the ship was used purely for carrying stores for other aircraft carriers in the Pacific. As she was crewed mainly by reservists, the officers eased off a little. One of the ratings was, we were told, a survivor from *HMS Hood*, and was very noticeable for his almost circular beard; in fact I think his beard was just about the largest I have ever seen.

The sailors taught us Shinty – a deck game played throughout the navy when there was enough space. It was akin to hockey, only a darn sight rougher, and heaven help you if you got your legs in the way of your opponents stick! Quite a few bandsmen had sore shins after this trip.

I was also introduced to the navy habit of smoking 'ticklers'. First you bought an eight ounce tin of Wills *Birdseye* tobacco and a packet of cigarette papers, then set to and rolled your own. I must admit I've never tasted a sweeter cigarette and if I could purchase *Birdseye* today, I could easily take up smoking again!

During the night we heard a pipe: 'No smoking on the upper

or open decks of the ship.'

It seemed we were being shadowed by an unidentified aircraft and the captain was taking no chances.

It was decided to repay the crew's hospitality with perform-ances by both the military and dance bands. This we did from one of the aircraft lifts. We made our way to the hanger deck where, under the guidance of one of the ship's officers, we set up within the area of the lift and were then raised to within about four feet of the flight deck This enabled the ships crew to assemble around the edge in fact some even sat on the edge with their feet hanging over the side. The crew seemed to ap-preciate our performance but then anything that broke the monotony of life at sea was welcome.

We were informed that we would be playing the ship in when we reached harbour, so we set about blancoing, polishing, and generally smartening things up. We were busying ourselves with this chore when a Marine bugler appeared in the hatchway and blew the 'still' (a single note G), at which the bandsman next to me called out, 'Flat!'

Instantly, a roar came from the direction of the hatchway. 'I'll give you flat!'

The voice belonged to the ship's Master-at-Arms (police chief), who went on to inform us pongos that the captain was carrying out his inspection. The captain was not pleased to be greeted with such flippancy, but, as we were mere pongos, he gave us a piece of advice: 'My Marines carry out their blancoing in the heads.'

I must admit, after this incident we kept a fairly low profile

As *Warrior* approached the harbour at Sasebo, near Nagasaki in south western Japan, we formed up on the flight deck with a lieutenant in attendance, whose job it was to tell the bandmaster when to stop the band playing, so as to allow *Warrior* to exchange salutes with those we were passing. I think the longest we played was six or seven minutes.

While we were on deck we were able to watch the procedure called 'Buoy jumping'. A launch was dispatched from the ship's side carrying a sailor, who on reaching the designated buoy, would move from the launch onto the buoy and prepare the ring of the buoy to receive the screw shackle of the ship's mooring cable. An important part of this procedure relied on an officer standing right at the front of the flight deck holding a red flag, which he would raise to signal to the bridge when the ship's engines were to be stopped, leaving sufficient 'way' on the ship to reach the buoy without smashing into it.

Apparently there had been occasions when a sailor on such a buoy has had to jump for his life. Needless to say the officer was not the sailor's best friend. The ceremonials over, when the ship had come to rest in the middle of the harbour, we were told that a landing barge would be coming alongside to take us and our gear to the landing dockside in fifteen minutes! This meant a quick dash to the mess deck to collect all our belongings then another dash to the hanger deck, where a supplies door had been opened to allow the transfer to take place. The barge was alongside, and we started to 'cross load' (as the naval expression has it).

No problem..... except there was a drop of some 6' to the top of the barge, and a further 5' to the bottom of the barge! We were all still dressed in our best, plus white belts and so on. We were none to happy and, as was my way in those days, I gave free vent to my feelings. The Band Sergeant told me to shut up, but nothing more. It was my guess that he felt much the same as we did. When the loading was finished the barge transported us across the harbour to a loading dock where some American 6x6 lorries were waiting for us. Once we'd loaded ourselves and our gear into these, they whisked us away to a railway station.

We piled all our kit on the platform indicated, to await the arrival of the train which was to carry us on to the town of Kure, a port beyond Hiroshima on the main island of Honshu. Being military persons we either hunted around for something to eat and drink or just made ourselves comfortable and had a kip. The train eventually arrived with an official who spoke a little English but, with a great deal of hand signalling and lots of bowing, got across to us that this was our train. We boarded it and made ourselves comfortable although some made themselves too comfortable and soon became wrapped in the arms of Morpheus, missing the night landscape of Japan as we were transported across the Southern Peninsular to Kure.

On the outskirts of Kure was situated the JRBD (Japan Reinforcement Base Depot) which was the principal British base in this area. Like any base of this type it was staffed by personnel whose former units had found them dispensable and for whom they wanted to find Extra-Regimentally

Employed posts. There were other camps in the area containing Canadians, Australians, and New Zealanders and from time to time the rivalry between nations could get out of hand. To keep things on an even keel, Military Police patrols consisting of one MP from each country were on duty most nights. It seemed to work!

While awaiting our next move, we learned that Randolph Turpin had won the World Middleweight Boxing Championship. We were amazed that in a matter of days we were watching the fight on the silver screen. Someone, somewhere must really have got their finger out and made this a priority!

If you wanted to make any purchases in the town you made your way to a small side window of the Pay Office at 17:00hrs. Here you handed over your BAFS (British Armed Forces money) notes to the value you wanted and received Japanese Yen in exchange. I noticed that one always received Yen notes, never any coinage, even though the official exchange rate declared a precise amount of Yen to the pound. Characteristically, I enquired why this was so and was informed that the small amounts in coins were placed in a fund for the poor children in the area. I realised there was no point in arguing the toss, or pressing the matter but I'm willing to bet that the 'poor' pay clerks rarely paid for their extras out of their own pockets. Such was life in this sort of establishment!

I have always had an interest in military medals and decorations and one evening while browsing in one of the local shops I was offered a complete set of medals of the *Order of the Rising Sun.* It was complete in every detail but as we were heading into a war zone and anything could happen I decided against buying the medals.

While we were there, the one thing that nearly drove us insane was a tune called *China Nights*, which was played or sung every hour of the day or night while we were in Japan. To really rub it in, the bandleader, Billy Cotton took the tune and had an arrangement made of it called *Moon over Malaya*, which became very popular about the time the battalion came home. We seemed to be haunted by this tune.

During our stay in Kure we discovered a restaurant run by the Australians, where they served fresh milk! Needless to say we overindulged and paid the penalty. One of the Japanese girls serving in the restaurant was a survivor of the Atomic Bomb attack on Hiroshima. She had a slight limp and would tell us only a small part of her experience but never all her story. (I sometimes wonder if she survived the years.)

While at the JRBD we received not only booster inoculations but also injections against elephantiasis. To receive these, we paraded at the door of the designated hut with our sleeves rolled higher than normal with our AB64, Part One in hand.

I stepped into the hut, handed over my pay book and received a jab in one arm, then as instructed, continued through the hut. Halfway along, I received another jab in the other arm. On reaching the exit door I was given my AB64, duly signed to the effect I'd received the stated inoculation.

One day a soldier approached me and after the usual pleasantries, asked me if I had any use for a pair of American fur lined flying boots.

'If the price is right, I might think about it,' I said guardedly.

'How about two packets of fags?'

'OK,' I agreed, with which he disappeared into a nearby hut and came out a moment later carrying the boots. I handed over the cigarettes and became the new owner of the boots. I suppose I should have given the matter a little more thought but, what the heck, tomorrow held I knew not what!

I decided to send the boots to my home address. I obtained a cotton pillow case, wrapped the boots in the cloth, sowed the whole into a fair parcel, wrote my home address on the cloth and made my way to the Forces Post Office on the camp and duly despatched my ill-gotten gains. The bundle duly arrived intact and awaited my return. If only I'd had the courage to have done this with the *Order of the Rising Sun*!

CHAPTER EIGHT

To war with crotchets and quaver.

We were transported to the docks in Kure, where we looked around for whichever wonderful ship was to whisk us away to war. The only craft in sight was a Tank Landing Ship, called the *Sir Charles McCleod*, which turned out to be our magic carpet.

This vessel was manned by a number of Royal Engineers and Royal Army Service personnel although the officers were Merchant Navy, with one 'four ringer' on the bridge and another in the engine room. Judging by conversations overheard, they didn't enjoy a cordial relationship! This Tank Landing Ship was 327' long and weighed 4,000 tons. Being flat-bottomed it was very difficult to handle in any kind of running sea. An LST had loading doors and a ramp at the front, an area through the centre of the vessel for carrying vehicles – on this voyage three tanks, two 3-ton lorries and various smaller vehicles. Down either side of the vessel were small cabins containing three or four bunks. The bridge and engine room were situated at the rear of the ship, as were the living quarters of the personnel manning the ship.

Once on board the *Sir Charles McCleod*, we asked the

inevitable question. 'What's the crossing like?'

'Smooth as silk,' replied a Corporal of Engineers. 'Five or six hours.'

We cast off and all went well until we left the sheltered waters between the islands of Honshu and Kyshu. The wind started to increase, as did the swell. The ship, being flat-bottomed, rode up the swell, rather than pushing through it, and as she went over a crest, the propellers would come out of the sea and spin at an alarming rate. The corporal of 'the smooth as silk', was amongst the first to succumb and didn't surface again until eventually we docked in Pusan!

I say 'eventually' as we'd spent some time cruising up and down the Korean coast. At one time I was told (though I can't vouch for the truth of it) that the captain was looking for two white lights that marked the entrance to Pusan harbour. In the end we got in and docked. Here military logic again raised its head when all the tanks and vehicles were offloaded to be replaced about three hours later by an identical cargo. It seems this procedure had to be carried out because the numbers on the paperwork did not match those held by the controlling office! So rather than change the numbers on the paperwork the load had to be changed (despite the patent waste of time and money).

We set sail for Inchon, where, on arrival, the LST 'ran up' the beach, and the ship's cable was looped over one of the baulks of timber attached to chains secured in the pebble beach. We had to run high up the beach because there was a twelve foot difference between low and high tides, as the

Americans had discovered when they'd carried out their amphibious landings earlier in the war, and left a lot of their landing craft stranded on the breakwater.

Just after we had tied up, a South Korean LST ran in alongside the *Sir Charles McCloed* and looped her mooring line over the same timber, and over our line. All was well until the tide started to drop. What happened then was the South Korean LST started to slip back, her cable tightened, thereby snapping the timber which caused both vessels to float from the shore. The South Korean skipper got into a panic, ordered his winchman to take in his cable, with the result that both the vessels were drawn together bow to bow, and as they both had their loading doors open and ramps down they met with an almighty clang.

The captain of the *Sir Charles McCloed* became very vocal and if the South Korean skipper had any doubts about his parentage, he had them cleared up at that point!

Eventually, we disembarked, climbed aboard some Canadian driven 6x6 American lorries and were transported to the battalion "B" Echelon, situated alongside a village called Uijonbu (Wee jon boo), north of Seoul. En route most of the lorries lost their wing mirrors, smashed by lorries driven by Americans travelling in the opposite direction. It seemed that this was the sport of the season amongst the drivers.

As we drove into the camp we were greeted by a large sign bearing the words 'KNELLER HALL' with the Commonwealth divisional sign on one side and the Brigade sign on the other.

The RSM who had arranged the provision of a marquee for our use and had the sign painted, was there to greet us. He proceeded to give us all sorts of friendly advice, such as the positioning of the stores, cookhouse and toilets. The toilets were of the thunder box variety and were situated on the top of a knoll, surrounded by a circle of bushes which provided some sort of privacy and also stopped the locals from being offended by our European habits. These thunder boxes were placed over very deep holes which were not only receptacles of human waste but also of waste oil and such like, so as to prevent possible infections. This latter gave rise to an incident which was very entertaining for those watching, if not for the man concerned.

One day a squaddie made his way up to the knoll with the latest English newspaper, no doubt intending to get a few minutes' peace and quiet to catch up with recent news and gossip from home. After settling in, he lit a cigarette then cast the lighted match down the hole. The resulting eruption looked similar to those seen on cinema screens when films of the Atomic Bomb explosions are shown. How the squaddie broke through the encircling bushes I do not know, especially as his trousers were down around his ankles!

One day a jeep appeared with the inscription FYJI'MA just below the windscreen. This vehicle belonged to the Commanding Officer and the inscription meant *F—— You Jack I'm Alright* and proved to be a real morale booster, especially when things were getting difficult.

A SHROPSHIRE BOY

Our living quarters had no beds which meant we very quickly learned to improvise with four blankets and a poncho, which I used in the following manner: I took one blanket and laid it lengthways on the poncho, then took another, folded it over three times, following this with a third blanket, again folded, which I placed over the others before finally enfolding the whole with the blanket first laid on the poncho, after folding in the bottom of the blankets so as to form a sleeping bag. The poncho was then brought over to form a damp-proof cover.

There was a plus side to this bedless existence. Every time we went out, we had somewhere to hide our beer and personal items. It became normal to see the bandsmen on their return probing the floor area to retrieve their goods; even in a war zone there were sticky fingers around! Beer (Japanese *Ashai*) was available on payment at the QM stores. You could buy almost as much as you wanted and as the band travelled into the 'dry' American zone, it seemed a good opportunity to provide not only comfort to our allies but also make a bob or two.

We settled in and started on the work we had come to Korea to do. We were destined to travel extensively, not only throughout the Commonwealth Division area, but also into the neighbouring American sectors, in which there were soldiers from Greece, Turkey and Belgium, among others.

Our sorties into the American sector brought about an incident I shall never forget. The band, aboard 3-ton lorries, were going to an area known as Swing Forward, and as we travelled along the MSR (Main Supply Route) we became aware that the American 155mm Howitzers (Long Toms) were firing at a terrifically furious rate. We swung off the MSR to enter the camp where we were to perform and as we drove in, one of the 3-tonners slid sideways and got its canopy stuck under the branch of a tree. While the drivers and various Americans were sorting this out, a command car (slightly bigger than a jeep but smaller than a 15cwt) arrived behind us. On board was a Two-star General who commenced to yell at everyone in sight.

"STRANGE BLOKES THESE YANKS" CHARLIE."

'I've got men cut off up there. So get this Goddam truck outa here!'

Quite what difference our truck made to the situation I never fathomed! The general might have done a better to take to his feet and walk wherever he wanted to get to in the camp! I doubt if we helped by sitting in the lorry grinning like Cheshire cats. Eventually someone produced a chain-saw, cut through the branch and nearly everyone was happy.

As always, we were asked if we wanted 'chow', and since the American rations always seemed better than ours, we accepted with great enthusiasm. We were shown where the mess hall was situated and told to go and 'enjoy'. As we approached the mess tent we saw two men standing some distance apart from each other, but obviously waiting to be served. Being British we formed a tight packed queue behind the second man.

There came an almighty shout from the direction of the mess tent. 'What the hell do you think you're doing? GET SPREAD OUT!'

It seems the American army stand in 'line' with a space of yards between each man to reduce the possibility of casualties if any shells drop in the area.

Having eaten we gave our performance which included some old Music Hall songs. I sang *If you were the only girl in the World*, while another bandsman took the part of the girl, suitably attired, and it went over quite well. (I thank goodness I had at this time grown quite a substantial moustache therefore couldn't have taken any female part.)

The Olde Bull and Bush had props which included a tray, complete with glasses and a bottle. During this rendition there were shouts from the audience, 'Got any full ones?' and various other requests for drinks.

After the show those making the enquiries came to the area

where we were packing away our instruments and I believe a lively exchange took place, as a result of which one or two of our members ended up some what wealthier. Our visit over, we loaded our kit and drove a reverse journey along the side road towards the MSR. While travelling along this road in the pale moonlight we saw lots of faces looking up as we passed but we took little notice. Back at our 'B' Echelon we were greeted by the RSM who informed us that the adjutant was most concerned, as they'd been told that Swing Forward had been cut off by enemy forces. I think we were lucky that night!

Our journeys around Korea took us from North of the Imjin River to Pusan in the South, via Taegu & Seoul in the centre. There seemed little of South Korea we did not pass over at some time or other either by road or by air.

One of the most interesting journeys we made was to entertain the New Zealand gunners, who according to the sharp-end wallahs were the best in the world when it came to the 25 pounders. Some said they could make the guns sing! We left our base in the usual 3-tonners and after some time realised we were travelling over new ground and seemed to be heading away from the Commonwealth Division lines, in the general direction of the Imjin river. We were driven down a track with minefields either side to a point where there was a gap in the rather extensive barbed wire at which stood a solitary figure who turned out to be a Red Cap. He directed us towards the position of the guns. As we started to move away the MP asked if anybody had a cigarette to spare. I doubt if I shall ever again see so many cigarettes in the air at the same time.

The reason for the guns being so far away from their 'pits' was that the gunners wanted to get a little more range into enemy territory and the only way was to move outside the wire. We gave our performance, which was warmly received. (I have a feeling the Chinese had a listen and must have liked it otherwise we might have received a 'warm return'!)

On our return the MP was still at his post – a lonely life indeed. It was over this incident that I started to gain a respect for the Military Police. It's a pity it had to fade later!

One day we were requested by the Band Sergeant to give our brasses a little extra sparkle and our boots a little extra polish, in fact, look our best. We discovered on arrival at our destination that we were to play for an Officers' Mess gathering of the Northumberland Fusiliers. (The Northumberland Fusiliers were in the same brigade as the Glorious Gloucesters. In fact, the mess tent was pitched on the slopes of a valley then known as 'Gloucester Valley'.)

After our performance we were praised by the NF Commanding Officer, a very dapper man in corduroy trousers and suede desert boots who wore at his throat a red cravat held in place by a gold fox's head pin.

Once again I had that funny feeling that the Chinese had a listen to our performance.

At one point we spent some time in a transit camp on the outskirts of Seoul. This camp covered a very large area which, judging by the buildings, had been a college of some sort. The camp was surrounded by a very thick, high barbed wire fence the other side of which was a Military Corrective Establishment (or 'glass house'). Inside the MCE one could see a large, high mound with a figure of '8' track running across, up and down its face. You would see inmates stripped to the waist with large filled packs on their backs running up and down this mound, being encouraged by members of the staff. The staff came from all nations in the Commonwealth Division. Some of our colonial friends would hurl abuse at both staff and inmates but I'm afraid I chickened out as I had no desire to join the inmates.

During our stay here, we observed clearly the dislike of one culture for another. Among the transients were members of the Royal Canadian Artillery, also the Royal 22nd Regiment of Canada (The Vandoos). Most of the Artillery were Native Canadians (i.e: Indians) while the Vandoos were French speaking Canadian from the French Provinces. Most of the time they co-existed fairly happily, but on occasions their differences flared up and if you had any brains at all, you exited very rapidly. Clubs and knives were the order of the day.

It was here I showed off my ability at acrobatics, when I moved backwards, through a window (open at the time)!

To me one of the more amusing features of the camp was the arrangement of the thunder boxes. They were in the open and placed, as always, over earth pits, but in this case in a square with ten boxes to each side, and a grand sight it was when all the boxes were occupied!

One morning, while I was in residence there, an Australian came and took up a seat nearby. He lit a cigarette, opened a newspaper and settled in. After a few minutes another Australian came past and saluted (unusual at any time for Aussies), at which the one *in situ* took his cigarette from his mouth and returned the salute, but said, 'Good morning, Charlie!'

It turned out that the new arrival was doing it for a dare!

A few days after this we were to be transported by the American Air Force from Seoul to Pusan. Most of us were a little nervous as many had not flown before and certainly not with the Americans who had a reputation of being a little 'laid back' over the servicing of their aircraft. Before we boarded the aircraft we were assembled near the Dakota and issued with parachutes, then given instruction by a crew chief.

'Make sure your harness is good and tight, especially in the crutch, otherwise you'll end up singing soprano! In the event of your having to leave the aircraft in a hurry, grasp the 'D' ring and as you leave the door count: one thousand, two thousand, three thousand, then pull the ring.'

A voice from the back was heard. 'By the time I've counted up to three thousand I WILL HAVE HIT THE GROUND!'

It was the bandsman of tourniquet fame.

The crew chief cast his eyes heavenward and spoke very calmly. 'Get on board, gentlemen, and enjoy your flight.'

The Dakota had metal bucket seats, not very comfortable and chilly in the rear. Also on board was the Chief of the South

Korean Police with whom we chatted for some time. He seemed a very pleasant chap and before we parted company he gave me his card which I kept for years just in case I ever returned to South Korea. (You never know!)

It was some time after that we learned he was much feared by the people of South Korea and had a terrible reputation. In Pusan on that occasion, one particular incident comes to mind. It concerned two male members of the NAAFI who, for some misdemeanour had been placed in the guard room which was surrounded by the usual barbed wire. The pair of them decided to go walkabout. Their absence was noted by the guard commander who felt things would be better served if he let them come back on their own.

When they decided finally to return, they tried to climb the barbed wire. By this time the guard for the night had taken over and a sentry challenged them. They remained where they were until the arrival of the guard commander who told them to climb down and get into the guard room where he informed them he was charging them with attempting to break in!

One of our next engagements was at the British Military Hospital. We were billeted in warm, dry Nissen huts and enjoyed good food, hot showers and the opportunity to be in the company of females.

One of the performances we gave meant we had to set up on a concrete slope outside of the Nurses' Mess. Not a problem, until it came to the *Anvil Chorus*. To provide the sound of the anvil, someone had made an instrument consisting of a piece of wood about twelve inches square, two nails and two pieces of scaffolding pole 12" long, but cut to length to provide a 'clang' pitched at the same key as the music. The two pieces of pole had holes drilled in them so as to rest over the nails which had been driven into the board but only enough to provide a resting place. The intended noise of the anvil was produced by striking the metal tubes with a wind iron. This 'instrument' was placed upon a *chair, folding, GS*. All went well until the *chair, folding*, because of the slope, decided to do just that. The tubes jumped off the nails and rolled down the slope, missed all the chairs and music stands and finishing up at the feet of the BM. I think he was about to explode but softened when a member of staff (female) asked if the band would like to partake of some refreshment. Needless to say, we accepted the offer and spent some time in the company of the hospital nursing staff of all ranks. I became involved with one of the sisters but despite the difference in ranks, and some light-hearted banter and leg-pulling on the part of her colleagues, we were able to spend time together with only ourselves for company.

I lost my virginity that night and for years kept in touch with the lady. Maybe one day we will meet again and each see how the years have treated the other!

Upon our return to Uijonbou we once again entered the world of practice and more practice. In fact, I suspect the following incident was due to someone either getting fed up with our music making, or deciding to 'help the bandsmen out'!

We were rehearsing in the open when there was one,

almighty explosion. At first we all froze, and then, as though someone had given a signal, we all made for Mother Earth. The RSM appeared and announced that there was no need to worry, that the explosion was only some of the pioneers disposing of redundant ammunition, also, he was sorry he hadn't warned us. As we settled down again, we heard some very strong language coming from the percussion stand area. On investigation we discovered that the drummer had taken cover beneath one of the timpani! We found this absolutely amazing as this drum rested on three legs, about 20" long and set in a triangular pattern. How he got his frame under and through them I shall never know!

One evening, some of the band decided to go with the crowd and pay a visit to the Australian Base, where they had set up an open air cinema. The cinema had been dug out of a hill side and terraced so as to provide a clear view of the silver screen for all. The terraced seating was made out of empty metal ammunition boxes, filled with earth and placed in such a way as to provide not only a seat but a back rest as well. We took our seats and were just getting comfortable when the heavens opened. Luckily, we had brought our ponchos with us and when the people running the cinema asked if the showing should go on we all said, 'Yes'.

The film? I shall never forget it – *The Great Caruso*.

I think in the band we really got to understand what was meant by 'United Nations'. We entertained at the American MASHs, Swedish MASHs, Field Hospitals of the British, Indian, Canadian, Australian, and New Zealand forces, to say nothing of the smaller units scattered around.

During the second tour undertaken by the band, once the winter weather of Korea had started to weaken, the dance band kept their instruments (including a piano) on the back of a three ton lorry and at the drop of a hat would go swanning off in search of isolated units. When they found such a unit, they would throw back the lorry's canopy and play for an hour or so.

Out of the blue one afternoon, the bandmaster called another bandsman and me into the Band Stores and informed us that we were heading home. We were to attend a Pupils' Course at the Royal Military School of Music, Kneller Hall, Twickenham – leaving next morning!

Our reaction? One of complete joy and a little apprehension as the School always held a certain mystery until you had attended at least a Pupils' Course.

We went back to our huts and dug up our beer and had a mighty farewell session with those who'd served with us over the past few years. I had a very thick head in the morning.

A P Sisley

CHAPTER NINE

Knock out your pipe and follow me (Kipling)

Korea set the British soldier a problem. The monotony of barren, forbidding hills, deserted villages and literally nothing to work on was a test for his reputation. But here the Tommy's genius for adaptability had flourished, knowing no equal among his allies or even among his cousins of the Commonwealth. He had become the object of their envy and admiration – so wrote one of the padres.

I can only hope that my small contribution had helped, and we'd been able to bring a few moments' relaxation into their lives, as well as a few moments' peace.

Our journey home began with our being transported to the main railway station in Seoul where we were directed to a train already standing at the platform.

'What time do we leave?'

'Don't know!'

Nobody seemed to know and nobody seemed to care. As we sat in the carriage we could see a huge sign put up by the United Nations on the roundabout just outside the station, warning our people to stay away from the local brew, along the lines – if my memory serves me right – 'Do not be tempted to drink the local brew. Three men went blind last week and several were hospitalised. *YOU WANT TO GO HOME? LEAVE THE LOCAL HOOCH ALONE!*'

We settled down, made ourselves as comfortable as possible, ate our haversack rations, regardless of when we might eat again. After some time two Korean railway workers came in to the carriage and with a mixture of broken English, abused Korean, and sign language we were able to discover our departure time. At this point my colleague and I decided to lighten our load and gave the two men most of our kit. We were not too worried as we could always say it had been lost in transit.

I wonder for how long the two railway workers went to work in our boots and jungle greens. We were both left with what we stood up in, a pair of PT shorts, our washing kit and writing materials. Why we kept the writing materials I don't know, as, apart from writing letters from the various ports we might call at, we had no use for them at all. We were able to pack all our remaining articles into one sea kit bag, with any remaining space available to be filled with duty frees.

Eventually the train moved out and we were transported to Tague. After asking our way from the transport office we were taken by lorry to the air base where, after checking in (and two pints of beer), we were informed we would by flying on to Iwakuni, in Japan.

Iwakuni was run by the Australian Air Force and on arrival

we were taken to the Mess Hall, which was quite an experience. As you entered the hall you were asked what you would like in the way of food. Upon receiving your request the man at the door relayed your order to the men behind the serving counter so that by the time you had walked the length of the Dining Hall, collected your cutlery and mess tray your order would be awaiting your collection, cooked exactly as requested.

One expression sticks in my mind and I have to be careful when my wife asks me what I want at home. This was the Aussie term for beans on toast.

The man on the door relayed the order in a bellow. 'Farters on a raft!'

After our meal we were introduced to the Australian crew with whom we would be continuing our journey. This consisted of a pilot, a navigator and a cargo-master, who took us to Kadena airfield on Okinawa. Landing there, we were taken for another meal, after which we were allowed to take a look around the airfield. It was like being on the largest Aircraft Carrier in the world!

Every type of plane you could imagine seemed to be there, from a Piper Cub observation plane, to the Black Widow (a twin boomed night-fighter) through to the huge B29 heavy bombers.

As we had no money, we were very much the guests of the American and Australian Air Forces and right royally they treated us!

Eventually we took off again and started on our way to the Philippines. About half-way along the planned course, the cargo-master came back into the hold and asked me (as my colleague was asleep) if I would like to go up front. I accepted eagerly and made my way into the cockpit, where, to my amazement, I found the pilot with his feet on the control panel calmly reading a book.

He saw my look of horror.

'It's all right, mate,' he said. 'George is flying us.'

As I had been brought up during the war, I needed no explanation that 'George' was an automatic pilot who needed no human control. The pilot invited me to sit in the co-pilot's seat. When I had settled in, an inevitable barrage of questions on my part set in, and I learned a lot about the instrument panel. This in turn led the pilot to ask if I would like to have a go at flying the aircraft.

'Yes,' I answered eagerly, but had to admit to some feelings of apprehension.

After I'd put my feet on the rudder pedals and my hands on the joystick as instructed, the pilot took his own hands off. 'You have control.'

To say we lost a lot of height in a very small space of time would be an understatement!

The pilot took back control with a rueful grin. 'Not to worry, everyone does that first time.'

The navigator stuck his head round the cockpit door but retired again when he realised what was going on. I took control again and managed to fly straight and level for some considerable distance over the Pacific Ocean towards Luzon. (I must, one day, find out how much a Dakota cost at the time.)

On reaching Luzon we landed on Clark Field, which in common with many American military installations, was named after one of their war heroes, in this case a fighter ace of the Pacific campaign. As always, the place carried all the American polish and flair.

We disembarked and made our way to yet another Mess Hall. After a few minutes the cargo-master came to tell us that the aircraft was not 100%. (I hoped it wasn't due to my flying.) He was very apologetic but told us we would be staying at least overnight in an American military hotel on the base.

The room we occupied was really comfortable and beautifully equipped, with everything from bath salts, to hair brushes and shoe brushes! We both had long, hot baths to get rid of the Korean dust residing deep in the pores of our skin.

After some time the pilot came to our room and told us he had managed to obtain a couple of US$ so we could at least have a few beers at the American Club on the base. This club was only a couple of minutes' walk from the hotel but as no one ever walked on American bases the pilot offered us a lift. The club surpassed anything the NAAFI could provide. We entered nervously and upon looking around saw the whole place was clad in dark red velvet and gold, even the chairs were clad in red velvet and the letters USO were embroidered into the backs. In gold!

We discovered that to obtain a drink you had to purchase a book of vouchers at a cost of $5 a book. This was outside our purse. (We learned later this voucher system was introduced to prevent any fiddling by civilian bar staff.)

As we turned to leave, an American master-sergeant approached and asked if we were British. We confirmed this, at which he asked where we had come from. Hearing that we'd been in Korea, he spread the information among the party he was with and we had no need to buy any beer for ourselves. It seemed he'd been stationed in Cambridgeshire during the past war and had fond memories of England.

Unfortunately, our aircraft was soon repaired, so we journeyed on to our next stop which turned out to be an airstrip carved from the jungle in Borneo. There appeared to be very little of interest in this place until the crew pointed out that there was an hotel set back a couple of hundred yards into the jungle. This turned out to be well-appointed and made a pleasant stopover.

While we were partaking of some refreshment there, we heard another aircraft landing but took no notice until a figure, dressed in beautifully tailored tan tropicals appeared in the doorway and demanded to know what we were doing in the lounge. This was the proverbial red rag as far as the Australians were concerned. Personally I would have thought that the glasses of beer which we were holding in our hands would have made it unnecessary to ask.

This character turned out to be a British brigadier (complete with staff, also immaculately turned out.)

Our crew were their usual laid back selves, and gave as good as they got while gently easing us out of the door and back to the aircraft to start the last leg of our journey to Singapore.

I soon realised that it wasn't ideal to be flying in a Dakota with a full bladder. The urinal worked something like this. On the small door leading to the very rear compartment there was a round, ball-like object with a hole about two inches across near the top, attached to the actual door as you faced it. A tube attached to this led down through the floor of the aircraft. This was fine for the men, unless you hit turbulence, in which case you got soggy feet, but I hesitate to think how the ladies managed!

We landed at Changi Air Field and after saying our farewells to the crew made our way to a hut marked 'Transport Office', where we discovered that no one knew anything about two bandsmen on their way to England. This didn't surprise us and after several telephone calls we were told to wait, and a truck would pick us up and take us to Nee Soon Transit camp.

We sat on the steps of the hut and waited but we'd forgotten that in such bases they rarely worked in the afternoon. It was about four hours before we were picked up and taken to be dumped outside a row of tents most of which appeared to be empty. Being good soldiers, the first thing we went in search of was the cook house (empty), then the office responsible for transients (empty). As no one appeared to be interested in us, we took occupation of a tent next to some Troopers of the Queen's Own VIth Hussars who were also heading home. We spent some time chatting and sipping beer before my colleague and myself both began to nod off, after all it had been quite a day!

The next thing I remember was one of the Troopers shaking

me and yelling that the lorry for the docks was due to leave in fifteen minutes! I can assure you we washed, dressed, packed what little kit we had, and still had a few moments left!

We reached the docks and started to climb the gangway up to *HMT Lancashire* when a Military Policeman on duty stopped us and asked for our movement orders. I produced our orders (pink in colour).

He looked at them sourly. 'These orders haven't been signed.'

We were astounded to think we'd come all that way on unsigned orders. We could have been arrested as deserters at the very least! I pondered the matter for a few seconds then asked the MP if he had a pen I might borrow. 'Certainly,' he replied and handed one over.

With pen in hand, I steered my colleague round behind one of the dockside warehouses where, using his back as a desk, I signed all the pages with the signature, '*I P Standing.*'

We returned to the gangway, handed the MP his pen and then our papers.

'That's better,' he grunted. 'Now go up the gangway, turn right at the top and report aboard at the Ship's Office. Have a good journey home!'

We obeyed his instruction and moved up the gangway as though the very devil were after us, determined that nothing was going to get in our way after all our adventures so far.

We were assigned to a troop deck which housed all sorts of Odds & Sods besides ourselves. These included a Belgian who had been the recipient of a napalm 'friendly fire' attack in Korea, the Trooper who had woken us that morning and a small Naval draft. There were other troop decks which were full of men, in the main heading home, but strangely each deck seemed to keep to their own even though they had mostly been brought together that day.

Once the *Lancashire* had set forth on the open sea, the ship's RSM came among us looking for men to perform certain duties. Most of the occupants of our deck heard him and what he was requesting while he was on the adjacent deck. Unfortunately I was literally caught napping by the time he got to me. I was informed that I would be performing a twelve hour guard duty every third evening on a corridor running through the area occupied by unaccompanied families.

This sounded a bit of a doddle, until I discovered there were wooden gratings in the floor over steps which led down to the troop decks. I took up my post in one of the lounges and settled down in an armchair from where I could see the length of the corridor. Every so often I could see fingers coming through the gratings in an attempt to lift it. There was many a plea for me to disappear (or words to that effect!). I informed those that would listen that I was not going to face ship's charges, but if they slipped through when I was at the other end of my patrol and out of sight, then that was another matter – as long as they said something to that effect at their Courts Martial.

The ship called at all the usual ports but after leaving Aden we sailed across to Mitisiwa (Massaswa) on the Eritrean coast. The reasons for stopping here was not only to take on men going home but also to allow a trooper of the Queen's Own IV Hussars, who was a Rhodesian, to make his way home on leave. I don't know how on earth he got back to his regiment!

The ship didn't dock but remained in the middle of the harbour, not too far from a floating dock and by sheer chance there was amongst the Naval Draft a Petty Officer who had helped to sail the dock out from England during the war. The troops we took on board were a draft from the South Wales Borderers who seemed all to be suffering from an incurable dose of verbal diarrhoea – at least, they ever stopped talking from dawn 'til dusk.

We sailed on through the Suez Canal, straight through Port Said into the Mediterranean Sea, without a stop, which made us curious. The following morning we were informed that serious rioting had broken out in Egypt but as we were just 'Odds & Sods' we wouldn't be turning back. The ship sailed on through the Straits of Gibraltar and turned north up the coast of Spain, then Portugal into a stiff headwind. If the number of times the same lighthouse appeared on our starboard side meant anything, our lack of progress was definitely of record-breaking proportions!

HMT Lancashire eventually tied up at Princes Dock (the very dock we had sailed from in 1949). We had re-entered the world of 'Hurry up and wait!' while the wheels of organisation ground their way. My colleague and I were summoned to the

Ship's Office where we were informed that we would not be allowed to disembark in jungle greens but would be issued with a Battle Dress for which we would have to pay. We protested loud and long. But to no avail. A 'Mexican Stand-off' situation arose, with us refusing to pay and the Ship's Quarter Master quoting King's Regulation regarding troops arriving from abroad.

Of course, we couldn't win and eventually had to give in as we wanted to get on with our journey. We handed over our pay books and in return received a very crumpled suit of Battle Dress with the advice that we might be able to claim the payment on arrival at our destination.

We dressed ourselves in our new suits and made our way down the gangway into the customs' shed. The customs officer who dealt with us was one of the old school, who asked where we had come from, and why we only had one sea kit bag between us. We told him the truth and he chalked our bag. 'Go and enjoy your leave, lads.'

As we turned to leave we realised that he was no easy touch, for he asked the next in the queue to up-end his kit bag. It seems that he had a suspicion which turned out to be well-founded, for when the man emptied his bag an American carbine fell out!

We made our way, via a public house, to the railway station and boarded a train going to Shrewsbury and I thought how good it was to gaze at green fields again. My colleague said he was going home before he reported in at the Depot. I could see the sense behind his thinking as he lived in Shropshire and not too far from the Depot, while my home was much too far to visit before reporting in, but I agreed to drag my heels before reporting.

On reaching Shrewsbury my colleague departed to his home, while I was left to kill a few hours before climbing the hill up to the Depot. I had a snack in one of the tea rooms, sat on a bench in the Quarry, and thanked my lucky stars that no one from the Depot passed that way on their way in to town and would become curious about a soldier sitting there in a very crumpled uniform.

CHAPTER TEN

Mithras, God of the morning, our trumpets waken the wall.
(Kipling)

I arrived at the gates of the Shrewsbury Depot just in time for tea, which meant my colleague was safe until around 9am the following day. I must say I was very happy to see him walk through the gates next morning. We reported in at the Orderly Room, and were informed that we were late, as according to our posting order, we should have been at the School a month before! We were kitted out (free), sent across to the tailor to have shoulder titles, 'Commonwealth Division' flashes and medal ribbons sewn on. Then we were dispatched to the Royal Military School of Music. To say we were "cock of the walk" was to say the least.

We arrived at the RMSM at Kneller Hall in Twickenham, just west of London, near the famous Rugby ground, and were told to report to the RSM's office in the main building. On finding it, we knocked and were bidden to enter. We were greeted by the sight of a musician from the Royal Army Medical Corps looking very downcast and a Regimental Sergeant Major of the Grenadier Guards looking very annoyed.

The RSM looked us over. 'At last! Some active service soldiers.'

I was tempted to look round at who had just come in behind us. The RSM dismissed the RAMC musician then went on to explain that the staff band musician had wanted to dodge a duty and had just been told that it was about time him and his kind did some real soldiering!

Although, of course, there were other pupils with medal ribbons, our arrival with campaign medal ribbons and divisional flashes was timely, to say the least.

The pupils were divided into companies, with each company being a complete military band. The companies were further divided into squads, each of which occupied a hut situated on the edge of a large sports field and contained either reed or brass, plus percussion. I was posted to 5 Squad, B company which was comprised of 'Heavy Brass' and a percussionist. In the squad was the musician who'd been in the RSM's office, and who was destined to become Senior Director of the Guards Brigade and retire in the rank of

Lieutenant Colonel. I met him when he was a student bandmaster when I made a visit to Kneller Hall some time later.

I mention 'Heavy Brass' because that was what I had become part of.

On reporting to the instrument store I was presented with the biggest B flat bass tuba I have ever seen. As I had reported late, this was the only instrument left. This bass was of American manufacture (Carlton) with a bell almost as big as a dustbin, and valves c.9" long! I can only thank my stars that my bandmaster didn't go out and buy one when eventually I returned to my regiment. It was an experience to play, but a devil to carry!

My next duty was to find which professor was to have the task of trying to improve my musical skills. He turned out to be principal tuba with the London Symphony Orchestra. I thought he would be a hard taskmaster but as things turned out he wasn't too tough. Most of the professors performed as members of the large orchestras, which often meant they'd been performing or travelling the night before. My professor's words still come to mind.

'Carry on lad, but not too loudly!' he would, say before nodding off for a cat nap.

This may sound as if it were an easy touch for me at the time but as I learned later, it had an affect on my grading, therefore my pay. The professors gave their tuition in brick built bunkers dotted around the wooded area of the grounds in the rear of the school. These bunkers were nearly sound proof, which was just as well because situated just over the wall were gardens of private houses. One could say that residents knew the school was there when they brought their houses but I'm sure they appreciated the efforts made to make life bearable for them. After all, their Wednesday evenings were disturbed enough throughout the summer season when the school held their public concert performances, especially with the gala concert every last Wednesday in the month and all the crashes and bangs of the finale.

While the school's director always conducted the finale, a guest conductor was invited to conduct a selected piece of music during the gala concert. Among these were Lt. Colonel Sir Vivian Dunn, Principal Director Royal Marines, Harry Mortimer of Brass Band fame and Sidney Torch, renowned for his appearances on the BBC. Sidney Torch composed, arranged, and conducted many orchestral pieces and on the night of his performance, to the delight of every one present, brought an arrangement of his called *And the Kitchen Sink*. This required one of the school members, in this case a student bandmaster, to march past the bandstand with a kitchen sink on his shoulder, beating time on it with a bass drum stick.

While the 'pupils' were at the school for just twelve months, the 'students' were there for a minimum of three years. During their time at the school they studied all military musical instruments, harmony, composition and arrangement of music. The students not only took military examination but invariably a civilian external examination which, if successful, gave them at least ARCM after their name.

A P Sisley

One of the students during my year was Captain Jane McDowell, who was hoping to be appointed Director of Music of the Woman's Royal Army Corps. Everyone treated her with respect tinged with admiration. It must have been difficult being the only woman in an establishment where all the posts, civilian and military, were filled by men.

The gala concerts always finished with such pieces as the *1812 Overture*, *Battle of Waterloo* and other items that required pyrotechnics. I remember on one occasion I was required to put the match to fireworks mounted on music stands behind the bandstand. All went well until the music quietened down. Looking along the stands, I spotted two fireworks we'd missed, so without further ado I applied match to blue paper and retired gracefully! The student in charge gave me a filthy look. That was all I got, but I believe he got a severe reprimand from the Director.

But were we not at the school to give the student bandmasters a hard time?

The commandant of the school was always a colonel. In my year it was Colonel Campbell Miles who was responsible for everything non-musical. The Commandant was assisted by an adjutant and a Guards Regimental Sergeant Major. These persons were responsible for the discipline of all military personnel.

The musical side of our lives was the responsibility of the director who held the rank of major. In my year the director was Meredith Roberts, assisted directly by the school sergeant-major, who was senior student and held sway over pupils and students alike.

Every squad was under the charge of a senior student who was assisted by another student bandmaster.

One of the greatest sins a pupil could commit was to leave a music stand or music either on the bandstand or in the practice hall. I managed this only once and when I went to collect the offending articles from the School sergeant-major's Office. I was informed I had been awarded seven days extra practice i.e: work from 5-7 pm in the practice hall.

Christmas came around and the school closed down for seven days but before this came into force, a notice was posted asking for volunteers to carry out work that could only be done while the school was closed. Those who volunteered would be able to take their leave when the school returned. I broke the golden rule and volunteered, although this proved to be no bad move. We were set to work at various tasks. As long as you had done a fair amount when the RSM came round on one of his not very frequent tours, all was well.

Someone came round and asked if any of us wanted to go to a Christmas dance being held by the telephonists of Kingston-upon-Thames exchange (nearly all girls in those days). A number of us went and a really good night was had by all, as far as I can remember ! How I got back to the school I DO NOT KNOW. The next thing I remembered was being shaken awake by a bandsman who had been sent by the RSM to inform me that it was Monday and I should have been on parade an hour since.

I was absolutely amazed and scrambled from my bed to find an empty champagne bottle beside my bed with an Arum lily sticking out of the top. I was still too hung over to start enquiries, let alone find out how it had got there. The RSM was quite understanding about the matter and sent me into Whitton to purchase some special crystals which we used to remove the tarnish from the brass rail around the conductor's rostrum on the bandstand.

The main body of the school returned from leave, which meant those who had remained behind could now proceed with their leave. Whether or not this period affected my future reports, I know not and at the time cared not a jot! Upon my return, I was told to report to the stores to be issued with the new No 1 Dress, which, for the Light Infantry, consisted of a tunic of rifle green with silver buttons, trousers of navy blue with an inch wide green stripe down the outer seams, plus a peaked cap of rifle green, black shoes and collarless white cotton shirts. I signed for all these articles, plus rifle green dress cords. This, at least, allowed us to appear on the concert platform although it was not the only purpose as we were to find out.

Some time later there appeared on the sports field the Director of music, the RSM, plus numerous student bandmasters who appeared to be joined together by white tape similar to that used by engineers to mark lanes through mine fields! The students were 'conducted' through various movements and manoeuvres. Speculation ran riot in our ranks but was forgotten for a while as other matters took over.

For my part, I took the opportunity to attempt my 2nd Class Certificate of Education. This certificate took in all the usual subjects, along with a paper set by the Director of Music. I must admit that my passing this certificate was rather special as, not only could I be promoted, up to and including the rank of Colour Sergeant, but also, which really pleased me, I'd sat the examination with virtually no coaching or tuition !

As the weather improved so did the opportunity to get out of the huts and into the sunshine. This gave some of the craftier pupils the chance to show their skill at getting out of individual practices. We noticed one pupil who used to go off amongst the trees that stood along the edge of the sports field and seemed to disappear!

One day one of our number said he was going to find the answer to this mystery. After the man in question went off towards the trees his 'follower' moved over to a vantage point which he had worked out earlier, and commenced his watch. After about a quarter of an hour the 'follower' came back, shaking his head and grinning all over his face.

It turned out that the skiver had entered the trees, had set up his music stand, but had not taken his instrument from its case. He did however, make sure the case was open, so as to be ready if one of the students came on the prowl. After some minutes he took a length of string from his pocket, closed his instrument case and attached the string to the handle of the case but first made sure that the string passed through the frame of the music stand. He then climbed the tree with the string in his teeth. Having made sure he was secure in the branches he then pulled up the music stand and instrument. After securing the stand and case he settled down fairly safe in the knowledge that unless he was really unlucky he was safe until the next meal time. These may seem extreme measures, but I think he should be given all credit for originality and initiative.

One day the civilian chief clerk sent for me and upon my somewhat breathless arrival in his office informed me that my belongings had arrive at H M Customs and Excise, Fazackerly, near Liverpool. As I had a leave period coming up, I suggested that I be granted a single warrant to take me to Fazackerly, and a further single warrant from Fazackerly back to Twickenham, via Bedford!

This simple request was met by various expletives. 'What do you think I'm running here? A Benevolent Society?'

The noise was heard by the RSM in his office next door and it was but a short time before he appeared in the doorway. He listened to the problem.

'As his belongings are being held by HM Customs and he's not responsible for that, but he is legally entitled to be in possession of said belongings and shouldn't be penalised by having to pay out of his own pocket for travel to collect his belongings.'

The clerk wasn't happy and for the rest of my time at the school played a very awkward game. However, I got my warrants and made my way to Fazackerly by bus and train only to find that when I alighted from the bus in the village I still had some way to walk. I eventually found myself in a large hanger type building in the company of a customs officer and a military policeman.

After I'd answered such questions as where had I last seen or been in possession of the wooden box and kit bag now arrayed before me, it seemed the customs man was not satisfied with my answers, while I could only tell the truth, and had stated honestly that I'd never seen the box before in my life, and had last seen the kit bag many months ago in storage at the Battle School in Kowloon. The customs officer then became quite awkward, even down to asking the MP to turn out the pockets of any civilian clothing to show any fluff, so as to prove the article had been worn.

I was then quizzed very thoroughly over some containers of 35mm film in the box. I told him I knew nothing about the film and assured him that I had never possessed a 35mm camera even to the point of giving the film to the MP! I was allowed eventually to leave which I did carrying the box and dragging the kit bag. I did ask the possibility of transport and was told there was a bus stop down the road.

I was lucky – a bus going in the right direction came along and although I was some way from the bus stop, the driver pulled up and the conductor helped me aboard and stowed my burdens so that other people wouldn't fall over them. As we neared Liverpool the conductor asked where I was making for. I gave him the name of the railway station where I wanted to catch a train going south for Bedford. The conductor relayed this information to the driver who took me to the nearest point he could and made sure I knew in which direction to go.

Eventually I reached to my parents' house in Bedford and was able to sort out any items of kit I didn't need straight away. This was done fairly easily as, with the uniform I'd been issued on leaving the boat, plus that issued at the Depot, I was now the possessor of three complete kits!

On occasion I caused some comment as I seemed to wear a different Divisional flash every time I walked out, in that one had the 40th Divisional flash, while another bore the Commonwealth Division shield and another had nothing!

During this leave I called in for a drink at a bar called *The Silver Grill*, where after obtaining a pint at the bar I looked around and saw, sitting at a table, a soldier who had been at school with me. We greeted each other with the inevitable question.

'Where did you get to?'

It turned out that he had seen my cap badge when I came in and was about to speak to me, but I'd beaten him to it. It transpired that he, being a signaller, had been part of the Brigade signal link attached to the KSLI in San Wai and had lived in the signallers hut two down the hill from the band, but we'd never met. Strange world isn't it?

Shortly after I got back from my leave, I met the girl who was the first to really interest me. There were always girls hanging about at Kneller Hall with reputations that were passed on from course to course. I soon became aware of them and although I might have taken a mild interest in one or two of them, I made very sure I didn't become heavily involved.

The girl I did become involved with was not one of those who habitually hung around after the Wednesday concerts, although as time went on she was to spend a lot of time waiting for the programme to finish and for me to join her at the gates.

She first came to my attention through one of the ex-Boys who had attended the School the year before me, and who was expecting to get married. As the battalion was due back in Blighty shortly, he'd been held back. One day he asked me if I'd like to meet his intended, and her parents. I said I would, and during the evening, a young lady, introduced to me as 'Digs', called round to see the future bride who was a friend (and, no, it hadn't been arranged!).

She caught my eye right from the start and, to use an old but apt saying, 'We got on like a house on fire.' It wasn't long before I discovered that Digs was just out of teacher training college and undergoing her probationary year teaching at a school in the East End of London. She was sharing a flat in Crystal Palace with another probationary teacher. After this first meeting we used to see each other after the Wednesday concert as her parents lived in Heston. Digs and her flat mate used to spend the night there then catch an early underground train to the station near the school, arriving with just enough time to arrive at the school for assembly (well, almost!).

It wasn't too long before I was spending Saturday night and most of Sunday at the flat, as her flat-mate went home to Wales on quite a number of weekends.

One day, while we were at individual practice, one of the others called over to me.

'I wonder why the flag on the church is flying at half mast?'

All sorts of ideas were proffered.

'Why not ask him, over there?' someone suggested, pointing at a man passing the gates.

Off went one of our number, made the enquiry and returned with the sad news that King George VI had died.

Again I had to parade at the clothing store, this time to be issued with Service Dress. We'd been informed that the Royal Military School of Music would be providing the finale for that year's Royal Tournament at Earls Court and that Service Dress would be required for rehearsal. Why we weren't allowed to wear Battle Dress I shall never know. We wore the Service Dress only once but I shall never forget mine. The jacket had green plastic buttons (at least I got away without having to clean them). The cap had a slashed peak and someone remarked that I looked like a 14-18 replica.

As always, with these events, there was a downside. We were told that there would be no music cards used during the performances and that the Director would be testing each section in turn. This may sound easy, but as the bass rarely played melody, remembering each individual note in turn would prove a little difficult. You also had to remember during this and the following period that your professor would still want his work to be covered.

We prepared ourselves and managed to satisfy the Director.

A SHROPSHIRE BOY

After a period of intense musical and marching rehearsal the time came for everyone to board a fleet of London Transport double-decker buses to be taken to Earl's Court arena. The route taken by the convoy took us through Twickenham, Richmond, East Sheen and Hammersmith. At certain points along the route a cacophony of sound bust forth from the buses, which provoked several dire warnings but as no one knew from where the instrument blowing started, and as nearly everyone took part, there was little the authorities could do but issue empty threats.

Taking part in the Royal Tournament did have its lighter moments. As I have said I had been issued with an instrument with a very large bell and as we marched up one side of the arena, the bell would overhang the boards of the seating area and members of the audience seated in the front rows would have to duck or lean back, although I must admit a few extra hefty lungfuls helped! I found taking part in an event like the Royal Tournament was a very worthwhile experience and I admit, despite all the extra work involved, I was glad I had the opportunity.

One of the institutions from my Kneller Hall days which I remember with pleasure was Ted's Café. After pay parade on Thursdays and before having to turn in for practice, during the winter months, a lot of us would make our way out of the side gate and walk five hundred yards to the café and there partake of what modern day dieticians would say was not good for cholesterol levels, and certainly not good for the waist line. There was a choice of fried egg, tomatoes (tinned), sausage (pork or beef), fried bread, baked beans (Heinz) – all or any combination of these with bread and butter, followed by a mug of strong tea.

It's surprising how much a fit and healthy young man can put away and I found it rather difficult to present myself for practice after a visit to Ted's. One of these days I must visit the area again one day and find out if his son has kept the business going although with all the reorganisation that's gone in, I doubt if the business is anywhere near as lucrative as it used to be.

It was while at Kneller Hall that my liking for the game of Rugby was rekindled. We used to wander down to the brook at the bottom of the sports field on match days, cross over, then sneak through the fence and stroll around in the crowds as though we had a right to be there, then just after the match had started we would creep through a hole in the grandstand barriers and make ourselves comfortable The amazing thing was even if there were members of the Royal family present nobody ever challenged our presence, perhaps because we were in uniform. I often wondered about his but never allowed it to interfere with my love of the game.

Although I sometimes felt that my presence and some of the other pupils, at the school was to make up numbers for such occasions as Gala concerts, I wouldn't have missed the experience, especially as it gave bandsmen like myself the opportunity to enjoy playing pieces of music that normally wouldn't be performed through lack of players – big, expansive pieces like *1812 Overture*, *The Wreckers* by Ethel Smythe, *Battle of Waterloo* and *Lohengrin* among many others. As I've said I was given the use of a real monster which, when called on to 'troll the depths', really made the bandstand shudder! Now the school has inevitably changed, I wonder if those under training still have the opportunity to find out what a tuba is really capable of.

This reminds me of yet another example of military logic. While at the school we sometimes had to give vocal renditions as part of the piece chosen, and the thinking seemed to be, 'If you play Bass, you sang bass; if you play cornet or clarinet then you sing top tenor; if you play saxophone or euphonium, then you sing baritone.'

Obviously, this didn't always work, and when it came to singing several bandsmen were left struggling to pitch their notes.

CHAPTER ELEVEN

The fear of strife and battle over....

When my time at Kneller Hall came to a close, I was posted back to the Depot in company with the bandsman with whom I'd travelled from Korea. However, before many days had past, along with the bandsman who'd introduced me to my future wife, we were posted to Whittington Barracks Lichfield, which the battalion would be taking over upon their arrival in the UK. The battalion duly arrived by train at Lichfield station and we were on hand to greet them as from the train tumbled (by order of course!) all the faces we had left behind in Korea.

It's hard to describe to someone who hasn't experienced this kind of occasion your feelings on seeing your comrades again. One thing that worried me was that the band were all carrying rifles! My concerns were soon allayed when I was told that the spare rifles belonging to the battalion had been issued to the band as this was the easiest way of getting said rifles transported home. The old saying, "Where there's a will there's a way," comes to mind.

The barracks were clamped down in thick fog for many days

and it was not until it lifted that we discovered that there was a clock on the façade of the building opposite, across the square.

The battalion plus band disappeared on disembarkation leave while those of us who had arrived in the UK early were posted to the Depot of the Oxfordshire and Buckinghamshire Light Infantry, situated in Cowley, Oxford. We were accommodated in wooden huts at the rear of the Depot with a very convenient lane running past which led to the main Oxford-London road. This proved very useful to me and two other bandsmen whom I've mentioned before. One was getting married, the other was my fellow traveller who had also formed a romantic attachment while at the Band School.

The weather at this time was brutal, made worse by a flu bug doing the rounds, which prompted the Medical Officer to issue an order that *all accommodation windows would be open at all times!*

It wasn't long before all our bedding and clothing were damp to a point that to get dressed in the mornings was quite a task. Many of us went down with very heavy colds but still had to carry out the same parades as the band of the Ox & Bucks. One particular passing out parade was carried out in such freezing conditions that the pistons of the brass instruments froze in their sleeves and no amount of blowing through the instrument would help. In fact, it was the moisture in one's breath that caused the freeze up.

A corporal in the Ox & Bucks band took me under his wing and attempted to give me instruction on the string bass A very able instructor he turned out to be, in fact, although I was not all that proficient I did play – up to a point - at an All Ranks dance after a very short space of time. I gave of my best. I coped in most of the numbers except for the very fast tempo pieces. In these I would play 'two in a bar'. This was soon picked up by bandsmen attending the dance in a non-playing capacity, and for a short period I became known as 'Two-in-a-Bar Pete'!

As we were more or less guests, we didn't fall foul of week-end duties and although we were not supposed to leave until after twelve noon on a Saturday, those heading for London found the lane very useful indeed. Some of the vehicles in which we hitched rides would never have passed an MOT Test, had it been in existence in those days. I recall one van in particular, on which, as we progressed towards London, the wings began to vibrate and the driver decreased his speed. I raised this with the driver and received the following in reply, 'When the wings vibrate, I know I am doing thirty five. When the wings fall off I know I've reached forty!'

Some say there was no adventure in the fifties!

After spending the greater part of Saturday and the whole of Sunday with my girlfriend, Digs, I used to make my way to Victoria where I would meet up with the others travelling back to Oxford by coach. Coaches were not only cheaper but much more convenient as the driver would drop us right outside the barracks gate.

We used to get some strange looks from the duty NCO when we reported in, as our names wouldn't be on the roster of those who had booked out that day, or the previous day, although I'm sure all the staff knew what we were up to.

A SHROPSHIRE BOY

As bandsmen from our regiment returned from leave they were sent to join us in Oxford. Little did we know what was in store for us. Eventually we were all posted back to rejoin the battalion in Lichfield where the first event of note was the departure of RSM 'Rocky' Knight, to be replaced by our old adversary, 'The Bird'. Many of the men were sad at the departure of Rocky as he had proved exactly what his nickname suggested. He was the rock upon which the battalion at that time had become what they were. They were efficient, smart, keen and able to work together under most conditions. The Bird was all together different. He some how lacked that certain something that the men of the battalion had come to expect of their RSM. He would throw his arms about when he got the slightest agitated and this habit was eventually to be his down fall.

While on the subject of postings, in and out, the NCO from the Ox & Bucks who had taught me the string bass was posted in to join us a Band Sergeant, taking the place of my 'friend', who went I knew not where and cared even less!

The bandmaster called me and the bandsman who had been at Kneller Hall with me into his office and presented us with our certificates from our course. He also advised us that my colleague would be upgraded to Five Star pay grade, as he had been classified as 'Very Good' by his professor, while I would be re-graded only to Four Star, as my professor had classified me only as 'Good'. I was naturally disappointed but the pill was sweetened a little when the bandmaster then gave me my Second Class Certificate of Education, which meant that if (and it was a big 'If') I decided to go for promotion I could go as far as WO 2nd Class. What was interesting was that my certificate was signed by the School Commandant, Colonel Campbell Miles. Usually this was left to lesser beings.

The battalion were scheduled to carry out 'Flag Marches' through a number of towns in both Shropshire and Herefordshire and were to be granted the Freedom of a number of these boroughs. As several men came from these towns, the excitement in the battalion was electric. This lasted until the rehearsals started, for not only did we have a new RSM but also a new Commanding Officer. This meant every a steep learning curve fro everyone, especially as the new CO was very much a clerical type.

Before the band and bugles got too involved they were to be issued with No. 1 Dress and everything which went with it. When it came to signing for these items I said to the Quarter Master that I had not been issued with these items here but at the School of Music, also that I had signed for them there. The Quarter Master informed me that I would sign for them regardless! It occurred to me a little later that this was how the Quarter Masters obtained their 'spares', while people like myself were made to look as though we had two issues!

The adjutant at this time requested that the band and bugles parade for a 'tailoring' inspection. It turned out that he had a thing about tunics being as tight as possible. This was to be the first of many such parades which meant that after a time the tunics were so tight the material between the button holes actually bowed when the tunic was fastened.

I was given the opportunity to demonstrate my new found

expertise by playing at an All Ranks dance. Everything went fairly well and I felt rather pleased with myself. After the dance had finished we were packing our instruments and stands away when a young lady who was rather the worse for drink appeared at the side of the stage and promptly passed out! It was decided that I would be Sir Galahad, and promptly picked up the girl. With her head resting on my left shoulder and chest, I carried her into a room at the back of the stage and set her down on a chair. I went back to finish my packing up. It was pointed out that there was a large amount of 'pancake' make up on the front of my tunic. Light Infantry Green and Goya make up do not go well together so I had to spend quite some time working on cleaning up my tunic. Luckily the result was passable.

The battalion made the Flag Marches through the counties with much interest and success. On the occasion of being granted the Freedom of Bridgnorth, on the saluting dais there were three descendants of Lord Hill who had been responsible for raising the 53rd Regiment of Foot which was one of the parent regiments of today's battalion. The other event of the day I recall was that the march off carried us through a turreted arch, down a very steep hill leading to the Lower Town, and I can assure you it was a very difficult task to play and put the brakes on. When eventually we came to a halt some joker called out. 'Let's do it the other way!'

I cannot possibly put on paper the replies he got!

CHAPTER TWELVE

Watch on the Rhine

March 1953

The battalion was warned for duty with the British Army of the Rhine

I was instructed to proceed with the advance party, for no particular reason that I could identify. I received the usual embarkation leave and elected to spend it with Digs. Doubtless there would be those who would say I should have spent it with my parents but I had been abroad before without any problems. Besides, as I hoped Digs and myself might become more seriously involved, I saw no great reason why I shouldn't follow this course.

Come the evening for my return to Lichfield, I said my farewells, then set off by bus for reach Kings Cross station but a pea-souper had set in and I soon realised that this was not the best course, so when I reached the first Underground station at Clapham Common, I changed my mode of transport. At Kings Cross I learned most trains all over the country had been hit by the fog and the only train on which I could continue was going only as far as Coventry, from where I would have to take my chances. In Coventry, after an agonisingly slow journey, I was lucky to find the RTO's Office still manned, so I was able to get my pass signed on the basis that I had made at least a reasonable attempt to get back to my unit. This was a relief as late arrival back from embarkation leave could be looked upon as a serious offence.

Along, with others who'd been delayed by the fog, I boarded a train going through to Tamworth. At Tamworth we were able to cadge a lift on the miners' bus, which was taking the night shift home and would pass the barrack gate. (This was the only time I saw miners travelling home in their pit black, as soon after this pit-head baths were introduced.)

I handed in my pass and never heard a word about my late return.

On the day before our departure, all the advance party were told to book an early call (03:30) at the Guard Room and to place a white towel on the foot of our beds to let the guard know who was to be the recipient of the call. However, there is always a joker in the pack, and the towel on the foot of my bed was moved across the room to another bed. It goes without saying that the woken bandsman wasn't too pleased and the ensuing row not only woke me but everyone else in the room, especially as the guard demanded a signature as proof that he'd made the call.

At the appointed hour, the party, under the control of a Colour Sergeant known as a bit of a ditherer, boarded a train back to London. On alighting from the train in Kings Cross we piled our kit on to a baggage trolley but had to wait for the Colour Sergeant. As we waited the Irish Mail came in on an adjacent platform at a fair speed, hit the buffers, mounted them and ended up on the roof of the newspaper kiosk at the end of the platform. We offered up a silent prayer of thanks for the Colour Sergeant, and his dithering.

From there, we journeyed on to Harwich where we boarded the overnight ferry (the *SS Vienna*) to the Hook of Holland. It was on this journey that I learned a very valuable lesson for use on future sailings on the route. If you slipped the purser a couple of pounds, you could have a comfortable bunk for the night, plus a nice strong cup of tea in the morning.

At the Hook our party was directed to board the Blue Train which was to carry us as far as Hanover where we changed trains to complete our journey to Gottingen.

In our party there was a corporal who at every opportunity attempted to introduce words of Korean into the German language He was none too successful but at least he got the attention of the girls. One other useful lesson I learned during this trip was that all European trains had a glass copula on the roof of their baggage wagons and the guards had no objection to any one sitting up there as it meant there was someone in the baggage wagon all the time. I found this very useful as I liked to pass the time reading or just watching the countryside going past.

On arrival in Gotttingen station we were met by a party from the regiment we were relieving (The Royal Irish Fusiliers).

They were waiting to help with the baggage and boxes, amongst them a bandsman who'd been in the same squad as me at the Kneller Hall. Small world, but that's how it was with bands in those days.

Border Barracks, Gottingen were situated on top of a heavily wooded hill on the outskirts of the town and proved to be unlike anything we had seen before! They'd been built during the German re-armament period of the thirties The barrack blocks all had triple glazing; all radiators had thermo-coupling valves while the corridors and ablution areas had grooved tiles on the floor so they could be washed down every morning without the perpetual hunt for some way of removing that last mop full of dirty water. The actual ablutions were tiled from floor to ceiling which also assisted with the morning clean up. The living accommodation consisted of large rooms which held twelve men. There were smaller rooms, holding five or six, while senior NCOs had a room to themselves. All living accommodation had wooden polished floors, which was demanding, but a small, price to pay for the luxury of triple glazing. (I often wondered why it took so long for double glazing to come into British homes.)

The kitchens were something to behold, but it was a long time before our cooks realised that what they took for oversized steamers were in actual fact pressure cookers!

As there was very little for bandsmen to do concerning the actual take-over, I was told I would be taking on the duties of Postman. This required my departure from the barracks every morning, except Sunday, at 07:30. The journey took us through Northiem and Goslar to an Army Postal Depot situated some two miles outside Goslar. Having collected the battalion's mail, both ordinary and registered, we would start back, stopping *en route* at the NAAFI in Goslar, where they served a wonderful cuppa and also gave us a dunking doughnut.

While partaking of these victuals I would place the registered mail inside my battle dress jacket, while the rest was left in the cab under the cold weather blanket belonging to the wagon. And I never lost so much as a stamp!

One very pleasant memory of Goslar was around Christmas time, when all would be festooned with lights hanging across the streets and the fairy lights and decorations glistened with frost.

As the barracks had been designed for Cavalry, the squares between the blocks were of a sandy construction and this proved to be to the liking of the CO as he very much enjoyed an equestrian style of life. However, he did get the top half of the square tarmacked under the pretence of having an all weather sports pitch.

One lunchtime we heard a strange "clicking" sound coming from behind our barrack block. Upon investigation we discovered the CO seated on a saddle which had been placed upon a wooden horse in one of the drained emergency water tanks, playing POLO! As the sides of the tank sloped inwards from outside edges towards the middle, the CO was never sure from which direction the ball would return. A brilliant idea but in the wrong place!

There was a barrage of ribald comments: 'Ride 'em,

Cowboy!'; 'Top marks, Jesse James!' and, 'They went that a-way!' issuing from the barrack blocks. Needless to say a dire warning was issued promising heavy penalties on anyone making such remarks in the future but I don't recall anyone getting caught.

Gottingen is a very old University town and just after our arrival some one discovered that the town had been founded in 953, thus worthy of great celebration.

Parades were organised with many bands, and floats depicting the town's many achievements through the ages although we noticed they were very careful to avoid the period between 1939 & 1945. I couldn't blame them for we, as an occupying power, were still some what of an unknown quantity. There was also a large Displaced Persons camp on the outskirts of the town, and any mention of the war could have had dire consequences.

The band was invited to play a program of suitable musical pieces to entertain the crowds gathering to watch the parade from among the avenues of beautiful trees. The people seemed to enjoy our efforts, although as we discovered, our predecessors were not liked too much. The Royal Irish Fusiliers did seem to have caused a lot of trouble in the town and we had yet to make our mark with the townspeople. While watching the festivities I got in to conversation with an elderly gentleman who remarked on the uniforms we were wearing and asked if we realised that King George II of Hanover was also King George I of England and, as such, introduced scarlet tunics into the British Army?

I had to admit I was unaware of this and was amazed that this should have been of such interest to a German.

While the barracks were on top of a hill, at the bottom was a very steep left-hand bend with the DP camp on the left hand side and a large house under construction on the right. One night two of the battalion's 'naughty boys' decided to take a spin in one of the three ton lorries. They descended the hill a little too fast, failed to take the bend and ended nose first in the side wall of the house. The lorry became firmly embedded in the house wall so the driver took off, leaving the lorry and its load (of rations) to the tender mercies of the Displaced Persons. (On a visit to Gottingen in 1998 I saw that the house had been finished and was sorely tempted to ask the occupants if they knew the history of the house.)

The next major event was the parade to celebrate the Coronation of Queen Elizabeth II. During this parade the battalion had to perform a *feu de joie* (Fire of Joy). This display was performed by the rifles being raised to the right shoulder with muzzles skywards and the left foot placed forward twelve inches from the position of attention. On the command, triggers were squeezed, starting with the right marker, followed in quick succession by the front rank The centre rank would follow and they in turn would be followed by the rear rank.

During rehearsals no ammunition was used so all that could be heard was the clicking of trigger mechanisms. You could safely bet that someone would be late! It was almost as though the offender had done it on purpose. The RSM – the Bird – just didn't have the same presence as his predecessor and there were still a number who remembered Rocky. The Bird would almost go airborne at a late 'shot', and if the offender was found, he would be sent off with his rifle above his head to run around the square until told to rejoin the parade. On the day of the real thing, I'm sure there were many mental fingers crossed.

The parade was held in front of invited civil dignitaries from the town and went well with no misfires in the *feu de joie*, although we later found out that those who had missed their turns in practice had the sense to keep their fingers well away from their triggers.

The following Sunday the band had to perform for a religious service at the Rhine Army Head Quarters in Bad Oynhausen. The service was held in the Grand Gallery, with the band occupying the Minstrels' Gallery. During the exit of all the generals and their staff, one of the Bandsmen gave a rendition of Purcell's *Trumpet Voluntary* and the acoustics were just right. I have never heard a better rendition.

One day shortly after this parade the adjutant ordered a fitting parade. The adjutant, with the tailor in tow, duly arrived but instead of being measured, we were asked our boot size. It seemed that some one had observed that when we had completed a movement, our trouser bottoms never fell back over our boots, so we were going to have a button sewn on the inside bottom of our dress trousers so that an elastic strap could be fitted that would pass under the instep of our footwear. He was also indenting for each man to receive a pair of 'overall' boots, as worn by officers with their Mess Dress, although these boots were never forthcoming in my time.

Someone, somewhere, realised that although bandsmen were non-combatant they were still a source of manpower in an emergency and if such an emergency occurred, we could still play a role of some importance; thus we were to be trained as War Emergency drivers.

Our role in an emergency would be to take over all available transport, tour the town picking up married families to take them to a designated port, then return to the battalion loaded with any ammunition as may have been required. Our training was in the hands of the Motor Transport sergeant and his NCOs.

On the day we started our training, we paraded in front of a line of 3-ton Bedford QL lorries. On joining us, the sergeant asked us to turn round so that we were facing the lorries. His first words to us have always stuck in my head.

'Gentlemen, the vehicles you see in front of you, unless handled properly, are killer weapons and you are about to become potential killers! I get very sick at the sight of blood. Make me a very happy; listen to what your instructors have to tell you. Learn to control the machinery. <u>Do not let it control you</u>!!'

(I realise driving instructors of today are making a living by what they do but would it be so wrong for leaner drivers to be given this advice?)

My instructor was the corporal next in command of the MT and as he climbed into the cab I noticed he had in his hand a thin metal rod which we later learned was a dip stick. He used this stick to great effect on our knuckles whenever we made a mistake either in routine or changing gear. Strange as it may seem none of us even considered for one moment reporting this to a higher rank, even though it was tantamount to 'striking'! The others on the course were carried in the back to await their turn behind the wheel and every time you missed a gear and the lorry lurched there would be an explosion of curses from the rear. However the curses were the least of an offender's worries as not only did he have to rectify the fault he also received his rap across the knuckles. There was not one bandsman who escaped the deadly dip stick!

After numerous circuits of the barrack perimeter we drove out at last through the main gate, descended the hill and drove into the town. On one of these occasions it was my turn at the wheel and as we proceeded along one of the streets, we encountered a brewer's dray unloading at one of the numerous bars. I gave it no more thought and carried on merrily.

The corporal took a sharp intake of breath. 'If I'd been rolling a cigarette, I wouldn't have been able to get the tobacco in the paper!'

In the centre of the town there was a crossroads with a set of traffic lights suspended over the centre. It seemed that every time our vehicle approached these lights they would change in our favour. It occurred to me, and one or two others, as a little strange but I thought nothing more of it until one Saturday we were in town and we saw a policeman operating a control box just around the corner from the junction and using the reflection in a shop window to watch the approaching traffic! Came the day for our skills to be tested, and we paraded with a feeling of apprehension about who we would get as examiner. My heart sank when I was informed my examiner would be the M T sergeant. We set off and I carried out the instructions as given but as we progressed through the countryside I suddenly realised that the sergeant was talking more about the Christmas trees than driving and kept asking my opinion about the various specimens we were passing. I ignored most of his questions and concentrated on passing my test. After a fair distance had been covered I was instructed to change with one of those in the back. As I climbed down from the cab, the sergeant gave his opinion. 'Not quite up to Brands Hatch standard, but you'll do!'

I felt really pleased with my effort. All the band passed their test but fortunately didn't have to do it under wartime conditions. I was really thankful as I learned that one of the vehicles we would have to drive was a huge diesel bus which the GSO drivers called a 1 to 5 – so called because when you changed gear, you had to count to five to allow the engine revolutions to die down before engaging the next gear !

On 27th July 1953 the Armistice was signed in Korea and the following facts emerged:

(1) The King's Shropshire Light Infantry along with The King's Own Scottish Borderers had served the longest of all the British regiments on active service.

(2) The Regimental band of the King's Shropshire Light

Infantry was the only band to have served (as a band) in Korea during the war, thereby making their medals all the more collectable.

CHAPTER THIRTEEN

Don't do as I DO.....

Shortly after my driving experience, along with two of lance-corporals from the band I was told I'd be joining the next junior NCOs cadre to be trained in the ways of a non-commissioned officer. We would still attend band duties whenever the cadre were undergoing weapon training or field exercises and so on. The cadre was under the control of a WO2 (company sergeant-major) who was known throughout the battalion as 'Button Stick' because of his regimental attitude. I found him a hard man, but fair in his judgements, also a very good tutor.

The three of us had just got used to the ways of the cadre when we were told that we were to return to the band. I never found out why, but as things turned out, it made little or no difference to me.

A couple of months later I read on Company Orders that my presence was requested at 09:30 the next morning. Full of trepidation I paraded, duly polished and brushed, as ordered. Upon being marched in front of the Company Commander I was informed that I was to attend the next Junior NCOs Cadre. I protested that it would be a waste of my time, as well as everyone else's, if the same thing happened as last time! The OC said he took my objection on board but none the less I would present myself at the cadre the next morning, to work under the same conditions as last time – that's to say, when the cadre were on weapon training, field training or RSM's parade, I would parade with the band, but at all other times with the cadre.

Next morning, with all my worldly goods, I reported to the barrack block set aside for the cadre where, to my surprise, I was allocated a single room. The big advantage of this was that I alone was responsible for the state of the room at any time. I could also shut my door and either work on my equipment or study during the periods that didn't affect me but didn't allow enough time for me to turn in with the band.

Every evening the name of the 'student' to be cadre senior next day would be posted. The cadre senior would take up his duties at Reveille and his first duty was to rouse all the other members of the cadre and ensure they actually got their feet on the floor. It was no good being awkward as everybody took their turn and, as the old saying goes, 'revenge is sweet'.

After laying out their beds, everyone pitched in and worked at the tasks allotted to them, such as cleaning the ablutions or fire buckets, floors, equipment, lecture rooms. As time went on one learned that time spent on the allotted task in the evening saved a lot of sweat in the morning. The cadre agreed that after teatime only certain latrines and WCs would be used during the night and only one bucket would be used for swilling down in the morning. When this sort of co-operation occurred, you began to realise what comradeship was all about. The cadre sergeant-major arrived at 08:30 every morning except Sundays. Upon his arrival at the top of the stairwell the Cadre Senior would call the cadre to attention in position outside their rooms and report, 'Cadre present and ready for inspection, Sir.'

You prayed that the CSM would not find any major fault, as he might then ask you to repeat your greeting, then place you on report as having told a lie to a senior rank! The CSM would produce from his pocket a pair of pristine white gloves, hand his stick to the Cadre Senior, place the gloves on his hands and commence his inspection, during which he would find dust and dirt in places you would have sworn it was not possible after all the effort spent on the clean up. He would call for a chair to stand on while he inspected the toilet cubicles, wiping his gloved hand along the back of the cisterns. If you were lucky and no dust was found, you would be advised that the chair he had been standing on wanted polishing, for which the Cadre Senior would receive a 'demerit', which meant completing a given task before next parade!

The CSM would carry on with his inspection, with the Cadre Senior in close attendance hoping to find out which item of kit/equipment was the CSMs chosen item for the day, which he never divulged until the end. The barrack rooms and the lecture rooms were all taken in and all received the same close scrutiny, even down to the hinge pins on the doors!

Everything that could be folded square had to be so. Spare boot laces had to be rolled in the fashion of a hangman's noose and then polished. Boot polish tins had to have the lid polished and shiny. All corners of the rooms had to be 'picked out' with the aid of a needle from your hussif, then brushed out using a tooth brush (kept specially for the purpose). All visible water pipes were burnished using three strips of material:

1. A strip of emery cloth about 1" wide, which you begged or stole from the MT sheds. This was scrubbed around and along the pipes until all signs of paint were removed.

2. A strip of cloth soaked in Brasso was used in the same way as the cloth before then

3. A strip of flannelette as used to clean one's rifle (commonly known as 4x2) was used in the same scrubbing way to finish off and you prayed that the result would please your superiors. (No chance!)

Nothing was spared. If any dust was found the Cadre Senior would be held responsible and he would have the task of chasing the others. On reflection, it was one way of showing the type of responsibility you would have to shoulder if you gained that precious first stripe.

No 'girlie' pictures were allowed to be visible. You were allowed one photograph of a personal nature, i.e.: family or girl friend. Some people today might say this was tantamount to bullying. I thought then and still think it taught you to take such things on the chin and then to get on with your job. I also think that to command others you have got to have 'been there, done that, got the T-shirt!'

During my time on the course I had to have a pair of boots

exchanged, which as I explained earlier means a lot of hard work on the new pair to attain the required standard. The boots I received on exchange were of South African origin and although of wonderful leather they were BROWN! My worst problem was finding a leather dye to change them to regulation black. Using my limited knowledge of the German language and the timely help of one of one of the German girls who was employed in the NAAFI, who happened to be passing the shop, I was able to obtain the required dye and triumphantly made my way back to my billet to start the work necessary to produce a pair of boots up to standard. With the dye, plus some 'spare' time I was able to do it; in fact the CSM took the boots and placed them in the corridor outside my room and gave the instruction that every member of the cadre was to look at them as they went past and to do some work on their own boots. I was not the most popular member of the Cadre for some days after this!

One morning, about 10:30 the CSM came into my room holding in his hand a 'Trip' flare, which had failed to ignite during manoeuvres the cadre had carried out the night before, and simply said, 'Get rid!', and placed the thing on my table. I pondered this for a few brief moments, then, with flare in hand and matches in pocket, I made my way down into the cellar area of the building. I entered one of the empty cellars that was open. I placed the flare on the floor, stuffed two or three match heads into the igniter mechanism, then struck the matches with the striker on the side of the match box. The flare burst in to life with a dark pink smoke which crept along the passage into the canteen area of the German Service Organisation and out of all the windows, yet nobody raised the alarm! I was a little concerned, but after things settled down I carried on as though nothing were amiss.

One Saturday morning, after RSM's drill parade, I had turned in for practice as the cadre was scheduled for field exercises, which meant I was not required. During 'tuning up', I glanced out of a window and saw the cadre being drilled by the Drill Pig. I rushed back to my billet, collected my rifle (issued to me for drill purposes and which I kept 'bright, shiny, and slightly oiled') and made my way to the drill square. I attempted to report to the DP, but was told to stand at attention on the edge of the square. I was kept standing there for some fifteen minutes before being allowed to join the squad. I was informed I would be charged with being absent for forty minutes from the designated drill parade. On Monday morning I was paraded before the Company Commander on a charge of absence. I was told that the charge was one of being absent from parade for a period of forty five minutes. When I was asked how did I plead. I replied, 'Not guilty.'

I was asked why and informed the OC that I had discovered that the evening before the parade the Drill Sergeant had issued verbal instruction that the programme had been changed but had not posted the change on the notice board which I had read at about 21:00 hrs, so I knew nothing of the change until I saw the cadre on the square. The OC asked the Drill Pig if this was so to which he replied, 'Yes.'

The charge against me was dismissed, *especially as I had turned in with the band.* The DP was asked to stay behind. After Orders had been dismissed I was told that the DP got a right roasting, and was told to make sure that any changes were posted on the notice board. Once again I was out of favour with the DP but very much in with the cadre.

During our training we had to give talks of interest to the other members of the cadre and take command of a squad at drill. We were also taught one or two 'wrinkles' which might help us in our future efforts. One lesson given was that if your 'precautionary' word of command is clear and precise, you can follow it with anything! You would be amazed at some of the words that were used!

One thing that took quite a lot of getting used to when facing a squad was that your left was their right, and vice versa; also remembering the position of the right marker after the squad had carried out a number of drill movements! Some of the drill periods were carried out under the supervision of the RSM and contained various movements that meant the squad finished some considerable distance away. The RSM would stand behind you and he would give you the moment to give a word of command to bring the squad back towards you. I know some of the cadre, including myself, were worried that their voices would not be strong enough to carry them through this period, but as things turned out we all survived.

I received a good report from my time of tuition and on the 24th November 1953 I was promoted to the dizzy heights of

A SHROPSHIRE BOY

Acting Unpaid Lance-Corporal. Someone once said, 'Lance-corporal is the hardest rank to achieve but the easiest to lose!'

I felt that having been there once before, albeit as a boy, I had, at least, a head start.

Christmas came around again and a couple of memories come to mind. The first was when the band and bugles had to sound Reveille, and the other was that my rank was posted as 'Paid' (a nice Christmas box). The festivities over we got back to the work for which we were paid – making music.

Although we did very little in the way of civilian engagements we did make recordings for the British Forces Network and also accompanied patrols, supplied by the battalion, along the border between the Russian Zone and ours. The word 'patrol' is not exactly fitting as we and the patrol would travel by lorry to the outskirts of a village, debus, then march (at Light Infantry pace) into the main square. The American patrol would 'march' in from the another direction. The two patrols would then face each other with bands in attendance and exchange salutes. Before the serious business started, the bands would play a couple of marches, in our case accompanied by the buglers. The Americans played a march by John Philip Sousa. After the formalities were over everybody would adjourn to a local Hostelry and spend some time drinking and swapping stories about life. I'm sure the Russians used to observe us from their watch towers and possibly laugh at our efforts to impress them and the local population.

As our position in the British Army of the Rhine was the most southerly, we made quite a few journeys in to the American Zone to take part in military displays and so on. The one which stands out in my mind was one in which someone discovered that the KSLI (53rd of Foot), the French 7th Hussars and the American 3rd Cavalry had all been engaged in the early American wars, and a 'three way military tournament' was arranged. The French gave a display showing an attack on a Vietnamese village. (I wonder if anyone thought of this being a pointer to the future?) The American display was one of armoured might. We gave a marching display, finishing off with the sounding of retreat. The organisers had invited a band from the German Service Organisation as they realised that a large number of Germans had served in the American wars. It was on this occasion that we realised that the GSO was the nucleus of the new German Army to be. I was fascinated by the cymbals which the German band used; they were the size of dustbin lids!

There was also a 'three way' tug of war. Someone had made a 'three way' rope, consisting of three lengths of rope attached to a central ring I forget who won, but it made quite an event.

We had been invited to stay overnight and as usual everything was larger than life, as is the American way. I think we all overindulged and awoke with thick heads next morning, but luckily we weren't leaving until after lunch so were able to get sorted out.

Our transport consisted of 3-ton lorries, which again brought into question the combination of the band and 3-ton lorries. As we travelled along the Autobahn, one of the lorries careered off the road but luckily chose a section where there were very few trees, and those were spaced far apart. The driver managed to steer a path that missed them. Afterwards, the sergeant in the cab admitted to being a little apprehensive and smiled a lot!

Whenever the battalion went on exercises, either battalion, Divisional or Rhine Army, I was detailed to carry out the duties of Post Corporal and although it meant an early start I was lucky compared to some of the duties the others got landed with!

Digs and I had for some time touched upon the matter of marriage, and as she was coming to Gottingen to visit the girl who had married the bandsman who had been at the Band School the year before me, I thought it an ideal occasion to become engaged. This being so, I had to put my mind to obtaining enough Deutsch Marks to buy an engagement ring from one of the excellent jewellers in the town. I had heard on the grapevine that one of the German drivers was a useful contact to have where the distribution of cigarettes was concerned. I was also able to become friendly with one of the German girls who worked in the cigarette kiosk who, every time I handed over the ration coupon which entitled me to a carton of two hundred, would slip my coupon back across the counter so that as I picked up the carton I also retrieved the coupon. I would go back to the barrack block, wrap the carton in newspaper then make my way to a pre-arranged spot and leave the cigarettes to be collected by the driver, who would then depart to I know not where and return with bundle of D Marks for me. Considering the driver was taking his cut, the sum concerned was quite good, and I achieved my required amount in a very short space of time.

Digs arrived to spend ten days in Gottingen and as this coincided with a spell of duty as Post Corporal we were able to spend most afternoons and evenings in each other's company, walking the woods around the barracks. In the woods was an hotel call The Kaiser Whilhelm Hof where one could sit at one of the tables which surrounded a natural bowl, and just let life pass you by. But like most things in life, it had to come to a close. Digs had to return to teaching while I returned to barracks but we both felt that getting engaged was one of the better things in our lives at this time.

April 6th 1954, I was promoted corporal so could look forward to saving a little more towards our wedding day. I started to attend confirmation lessons, which in turn led to my being confirmed in St George's Church, Hanover. As the British Zone of Germany was part of the diocese of the Bishop of London, the bishop himself carried out the confirmation. It was quite a day.

Another trip to Hanover occurred when a number of the band (including me) attended a concert given by the late, great Stan Kenton and his Orchestra. He was years ahead of his time and the sounds were out of this world. Anyone who knows anything about swing cannot but agree that the world of music lost a great musician when Stan Kenton died. I still have some of his recordings and play them from time to time, enjoying them as much as ever.

Around this time we received a warning that the band was very shortly to receive a Kneller Hall inspection. There was a slight feeling of panic, but the band sergeant put it succinctly.

'The band need have no fears as what we did not know now we would not know then and no amount of extra practices would make the slightest difference!' The sergeant would be one of those tested.

The day arrived with the Director of the School' testing the musical side, while the marching side of things were tested by the Commandant of the 'School'. I think a lot of the less wise learned a thing or two that day, the main thing being a band was responsible not just to the regiment alone. We passed inspection but couldn't help wondering what it was all about. We soon learned the answer; we were informed that there was to be a parade of the 11th Armoured Division in the presence of Princess Margaret and that the battalion had been chosen to provide the Guard of Honour. The parade was to take place on a disused airfield so we would be able to put on a show. I must have mentioned the RSM was not the world's greatest exponent of the English language and during one rehearsal was heard to give this advice: 'When you mark time, keep your feet still!' What he meant to say, of course, was, 'When you mark time do not move backwards or forwards.'

Another beauty was, 'She'll be coming in her own heli... heli....heli.... She'll be coming in her own transport.'

On one occasion the band and bugles came in for a blitzing, which gave rise to an entertaining incident. As normal, the band had arranged their march cards in order before parading. The RSM gave voice at the band sergeant who was in charge that day. The order was given for the battalion to get on the move, the band struck up and the strains of *Colonel Bogey* burst forth. The battalion fell about with laughter. The RSM went ballistic and threatened to place the Band Sergeant in close arrest. When things quietened down and the case of the march cards was explained, the RSM warned us against any further incidents of this nature. Anyone who has served in the forces that the march, Colonel Bogey has alternative, smutty lyrics, and the RSM, instead of laughing it off, threw a wobbly, only aggravating the situation to a point where it almost fell apart.

When the day of the parade came, all would have gone well, but it started to rain.... and didn't it rain! We stood in the downpour with white blanco streaming down the skirts of our tunics long after other units around us had gone to shelter. Eventually we received the order to stand down but to be ready to form up again at very short notice. We were told that the weather had prevented HRH's helicopter from taking off to which many replied, 'It hasn't done much for us either!'

This was the only time in my service I actually poured a large quantity of water from the bell of my instrument! Eventually the rain eased and we paraded in time for the arrival of the royal chopper. We performed, the lorried Infantry drove past, followed by the tanks, followed by our return to provide the final salute.

Easy? Far from it. The tanks owing to the soggy conditions had transported tons upon tons of mud onto the tarmac surface in front of the Grandstand, leaving great uneven mounds over which we had to march, playing. It may not have been the tidiest parade we have ever done but we received a message of congratulations for our efforts under trying conditions.

The wife of one of the officers started a drama group and I was asked if I would join the cast. I agreed and was given the part of *Rainbow*, the school caretaker in their production of *The Happiest Days of your Life*. The first night went very well and those attending said they had enjoyed it very much. As a result, I think we may have become a little over confident as the next night various cues were missed which led the producer to announce that at any future productions there would be a prompter, otherwise there would be no production! This statement was called to account when a request was received asking for a performance at Brigade Headquarters. We could hardly refuse, so press-ganged one of the bandsmen into being prompter; he did a good job, despite the lack of time to rehearse. We were, however, very worried about the set which was fairly fragile.

On our arrival at the venue we were greeted by a 'Rupert' who, as a member of the Brigadier's staff, fussed around the producer and introduced us to a member of the German Service Organisation, who turned out to be a carpenter. This God-sent German chippie asked what we required. Luckily we'd brought a copy of the play. This had a plan of the stage setting The carpenter took the plan and made a few notes on the back of an envelope. 'Leave it with me,' he said.

We took ourselves off for refreshment, after which we relaxed as best as we could. Half an hour before curtain up we returned to the stage and found the set built, complete with glazed windows, lights that worked when a switch was thrown, doors that opened when the knob was turned and the background lighting perfect. (I wondered if British workers could, or even would, have built the same in the same time?)

The performance was given in front of the Brigadier and guests and went like a dream – no missed cues or forgotten words.

As always, some tedious matter arose to mar our sense of well-being. In this case, a Brigadier's inspection. Since my promotion I had been placed in charge of boys and I passed on one or two lessons learnt on the cadre – for instance, to leave some small item, undusted, just inside the doorway where it would attract the attention of the inspecting officer. It appeared to work, as he made some comment but having done so, seemed not too particular about the rest of the room.

As the Brigadier was inspecting, he asked me if I was the person who had played the part of *Rainbow* in the recent very well presented production in Hanover?

When I confirmed that I was, he spent some time in conversation. He wanted to know, why had I joined the company? Were there likely to be any more productions in the near future? How did I feel about appearing before an audience?

The RSM was hopping from one leg to the other, the CO looked daggers and I was beginning to wonder what my future life was going to be like. One thing was certain, the Brigadier's conversation with me saved the rest of the band from a lengthy inspection.

My next venture on the 'boards' was with the band when we produced our own contribution to a battalion 'Smoker'. The bandmaster had discovered the manuscript of an arrangement of snatches from various operas. The only thing new was that the main parts were sung with words that had been arranged to fit the music and represented a Gang of Brigands. I played the part of *Antonio from Barcelonio*. All the parts were played by bandsmen, even the female characters. The show was a great success and greatly enjoyed by all, even if some said I looked like the CO's double!

At this stage, National Service was still in force, and there arrived in the battalion one N S Man who was almost at once promoted to L/Corporal and posted away to Officer Cadet Training Unit. On attaining his commission he was posted back to the battalion which was a very rare occurrence indeed. (He was to go into the City after his National Service and eventually became Lord Mayor of London!)

I applied for and was granted leave to get married. During my absence I had to hand the boys into the charge of one of the lance-corporals. This came as a bit of a let down, considering the work I had done with them but as things turned out it wasn't such a bad idea.

Digs and I were married in St Luke's Church in West Norwood and afterwards honeymooned in Eastbourne, where her parents were planning to move in the near future. It was during this time that we decided that rather than join me with the regiment in Germany, Digs would follow her career as a teacher. This may not have been one of our best decisions but it seemed good at the time. For the wedding, I wore my No.1Dress and of course the obligatory photographs were taken. When my copies arrived, the BM took one look. 'Pity you hadn't got your medals.You would have looked even smarter! (Our Korean medals arrived a few days after!)

Shortly after my return the band were granted local leave to be taken in Bad Hartzburg. This leave centre was situated in the foothills of the Hartz mountains, on the other side of which was the Russian Zone. I have never fathomed out why a leave centre should have been situated so close to the Russian zone, especially as we were always being told of the possibility of an attack by the Soviets.

The hostel was very comfortable indeed, the only snag being that the doors were locked at 23:00 hrs. This seemed an odd rule to me as it only encouraged men to spend the night out. One night, inevitably, some of us imbibed a little too heavily and missed lock up, so I decided that if the others gave me a 'bunk up' on to a sloping roof, at the top of which was a window, I would be able to climb through the window and make my way back to the front door to let them in.

I was given the necessary 'bunk up' and was making my way across the sloping roof when a Canadian voice came out of the dark. 'If you'd like to come down, I could open the door.'

I descended to the ground and was chewed over by a Canadian MP Sergeant who took my Number, Rank and Name, or at least he would have done if he had taken the protector off the tip of his pencil! The sergeant and two l/corporals escorted us to our rooms then decided to search the rest of the rooms. The room housing the boys was next to mine and the MPs found a girl in one of their beds! The l/corporal who had taken over the boys from me only weeks ago was charged. If he had been in another post, he would have received a roasting, but as he was in charge of boys it was decided that he'd failed to set an example or to show respect for his position. He was 'busted' to bandsman and I returned to being i/c boys for a short period while the whole matter was looked at.

Those in authority over us decided that we should be prepared in the event of a Russian move towards the border. In light of this it was decided to hold a rehearsal of what steps we would have to take if the Four Hour Warning was given. We packed all non-essential kit in our kit bags and piled them on the square to be burnt if the real thing came about. We bandsmen took our allotted place in the MT Lines but did not have to move any vehicles. Another exercise was on allotted days everyone had to wear gas masks and carry on with their allotted duties. This was all very well in the Rifle companies, clerical positions and similar, but how were we, as bandsmen and buglers, to carry on as usual? We compromised and held tutorials on the Elements of music or General musical matters.

At this time we received a number of '3- year men', and I made the discovery that there were thirteen members of the band with surnames beginning with the letter 'H'. I still think this might make for an entry in the Guinness Book of Records.

The band were not a fighting party but sometimes trouble came our way. One such occasion was during a duty visit to Bielefeld. The night before the parade for which we were there to provide the music, a number of us were seated in the canteen enjoying a pint. Every so often one of the RASC drivers from the unit who would be our audience kept having a verbal 'dig' at us. His mates tried to shut him up but he kept on. We ignored him in the hope he might go away. Eventually the driver made his way towards the exit but as he did so, he switched off the lights. I doubt if many could have moved as quickly as we did. In the short space of time between the lights being switched off and on again, we had got to our feet, removed web belts from around our waists and wrapped them around our knuckles and looked ready to take on the world. (It was bizarre that no one had said a word and yet we had all done the same thing! Comradeship?)

The driver had turned around in the doorway and as the lights came back on he hurled a steel chair in our direction. One of the bandsmen was not quick enough and the chair caught him a glancing blow above one of his ears. The injury was superficial but, like all wounds 'on the bone', bled profusely!

A SHROPSHIRE BOY

The driver was arrested and the last we heard, had been taken before a Court Martial and received a term in a Military Correction Establishment (Glass House).

Our next engagement of note was to be in attendance for the annual celebration of the battle of Minden by the King's Own Yorkshire Light Infantry. They were stationed in Berlin but their band was in England, so we got the job. Our journey started in Gottigen when we boarded a designated railway coach that was part of a train going to Hanover. On reaching Hanover our carriage was uncoupled and shunted into a siding This allowed the train going to Berlin to draw in to the platform for our carriage to be coupled on. After we were connected a sergeant of the RTO's staff came on board and started to seal every door with a wire around every door handle, held in place with a seal. Naturally, we asked why and were informed that the Russian's insisted on the sealing of the doors of all military trains before it entered their zone. While the Sergeant was explaining this he overlooked one door By the time we realised, the train was on its way.

When we reached the border crossing point, a British captain and his Russian counterpart boarded the train and together began to make their way through inspecting the door seals. Upon reaching the offending door the Russian blew a fuse! The British captain let him let off steam but at the same time asked if any one had a handkerchief. A handkerchief was produced and the captain proceeded to wrap it around the offending handles and finished it off with a perfect reef knot! The Russian

241

officer's attention was drawn to the master piece and he stopped steaming, broke into the broadest of grins and departed. (Strange folk these Russians!)

At one point in our journey our train drew alongside a Russian Troop train. Being British we did what the British soldier has done over the centuries, which is to make friends with those who wish to do the same.

At first the Russians appeared to take no notice of 'Hello, John,' or 'Hey, Ivan!'. They remained poker-faced and didn't even look in our direction. After a few minutes one of their number rose from his seat and left the carriage and those left began to soften. It was learned through sign language and their broken English that the one who had left was a sergeant and he had gone to the toilet and that one of their number was jamming the door to prevent his rapid return. Cigarettes and chocolate were passed over and at this point we felt that if the politicians left diplomacy to the British squaddies, there might not be another war.

On our arrival in Spandau barracks, the band were called together and given advice on how and how not to behave during our stay in Berlin. The main theme was not to get involved with the Russians as they were quite capable of making a major incident out of the smallest error.

We got down to the reason for our being in Berlin – *Minden Day.* This day was a major Battle Honour Day for the KOYLI, and part of the celebration was for all those taking part to wear white roses, for it seems that regiments involved in the battle had picked and wore such roses on their way to engage the

French in 1759. The drums were decked in white paper roses, while everyone on parade wore at least one of said roses. Those wearing peaked caps wore one each side plus one behind the cap badge. Those wearing berets wore one behind the cap badge. I kept mine for many years but they seemed to have got mislaid during one of our house moves. The French march, *Ca Ira* was played on this day, so the story goes, because while waiting to engage the enemy our troops heard the French bands playing it so the CO ordered our bandmaster to, 'Play it - only better!'

This march is quite tricky to play at Heavy Infantry pace but at Light Infantry pace requires – nay demands – some very lively finger work on the part of those with melody or counter melody. I'm glad to say, we survived.

Just down the road from the barracks was Spandau Prison, the sole occupant at this time being Rudolf Hess who had been Hitler's Deputy. It was he who had flown to Scotland to negotiate with the British, but his flight still raises controversy, even today! All visitors to Berlin had to visit Spandau if only to say they been there. The prison was guarded by each of the occupying powers in turn. During our visit it was the turn of the Russians. Outside the walls there were huge signs: 'NO PHOTOGRAPHY ALLOWED', in four languages. These notices meant nothing to one of our number, so up to the gate he strolled, with camera supported by a thin leather strap. Up went the camera, click went the shutter, crash went the picket gate, and out flew a Russian Officer, shouting in his language.

He grabbed the camera and with one jerk broke the strap from which it hung, hurled it to the ground, turned around and disappeared back through the gate leaving us standing there speechless – one with an aching neck!

When we related this incident to a member of the permanent regiments, he said we were lucky not to have been shot! It seems the Russians were very touchy over Spandau and its occupant. The band gave a concert in the city after which the bandmaster said as long as the instruments and kit were taken back to the barracks, the rest could stay and make their own way back. All very well, you may say, and all was well until some of the band decided to make their way back to Spandau by the *S-Bahn*. It seems they missed their station and decided to go on to the next station and catch the next train going in the opposite direction.

They were still in No 1 Dress and when they got up to leave at the next station, some friendly Germans made them sit down again and remove their peaked caps at the same time telling them that the station was in the Russian Zone and if they got off the train they would more than likely get arrested and thrown into jail!

Just after our escapades in Berlin we learned the reason for the Kneller Hall inspection. The bandmaster was leaving the Army to take up the position of Director of Music to The Southern Rhodesian Police and the powers that be wanted to see the new BM who would be taking over.

Once again the battalion was away, involved in exercises and manoeuvres, but for once I did not take over the duties of post Corporal as a consequence of which I found myself as Guard Commander with a l/corporal and twelve bandsmen under my control. Around 23:00 hrs one evening, there appeared in the Guard room doorway two of the wives of men out in the 'field', who stated there was a man looking through the windows of their ground floor married quarters and would I let one of the guard go with them to investigate?

The manner in which they made their complaint and their request made me rather wary, as a result of which I despatched my 2nd in Command plus two bandsmen with instructions to search the *outside area* of the buildings and to report back in fifteen minutes if nothing was found. You should have seen the faces of the two ladies. I can assure you they did not make any further requests/complaint at any time I was Guard Commander.

As it was now getting very cold during the hours of darkness the sentries were issued with ankle length coats made of animal skins, during their hours of patrol. These coats were really wonderful for keeping warm but I know of more than one bandsman who crept into the cellar area of one certain barrack block, from where, if they resisted the temptation to fall asleep, could see any movement on the part of the Orderly Officer or myself from the Guard Room therefore would be able to get out of the block by the time we arrived in their immediate area. One crafty lad was not able to make his exit in time so stood in the shadow of the doorway, then had the cheek to challenge us as we passed!

The new bandmaster took up his appointment just in time

for the start of the rehearsals for the presentation of new colours. Two things seemed to dog the rehearsals: Every time we got near the square, it rained! And the RSM seemed to have little or no control over the timing of the drill movements which drove the CO to call across the square, 'Let them find their own level, Mr Williams,' which is exactly what we did. It rained so persistently that it drove the bandmaster to write an arrangement of *It Ain't Gonna Rain No More* in an effort to bring a little humour into a very dismal occasion.

It was just after one of the rehearsals that one of the majors approached the bandmaster and said that he and some of the officers were wondering if all the trombone slides could go in and out together? The BM replied that this was possible but the result would be very discordant! The major walked away with out a word.

The new colours were presented by Field Marshal, the Lord Harding, who had addressed the battalion on the dockside in Singapore. The parade went extremely well and it DID NOT RAIN! In his address the Field Marshal commented on the battalion's presence and bearing. In a letter he sent afterwards, the Field Marshal said he had seen many such parades but never one better.

The band was granted leave in the UK. As we entered the barrack gates on our return, we noticed something different The NCOs were wearing different rank insignia, and their overcoat buttons were of a different design. The next morning we were to find out what it was all about.

A SHROPSHIRE BOY

While we were on leave, a directive had been received stating that all Light Infantry regiments would adopt the same insignia, i.e.: half-inch stripes in Light Infantry green upon a maize background. All badges of trade, rank or qualification would be LI green on maize. In addition, all buttons would be silver, with the LI Bugle only. At this time we did not realise that these changes were the first steps towards the formation of the present day Light Infantry, as part of the Light Division The new insignia and its background, plus Band Harp, plus Divisional patch certainly made an arm full! At the same time we had to change our cap badges for three quarter size and one of the boys had either lost his or had it stolen and it fell to me to have to take the boy to the quarter-master's store and attempt to get a replacement. Unfortunately the major quartermaster was still in the building and was not happy about the situation. 'I've had my cap badge for twenty years and have never lost it!' he said witheringly.

Before we realised what was happening the boy replied, 'But they were only issued this morning!'

Even I cringed at the resulting blast and beat a very hasty retreat!

Having reached the dizzy heights of NCO, it fell to my lot to take any extra practice sessions that were given. The BM had discovered somewhere copies of a German military march book and I liked to practice what little conducting skills I had, making use of these books. I'm sure there were those who became heartily sick of *Ich hat einen Kamerarden*, but I liked it!

Christmas Day arrived once more, and after the traditional Gunfire, the band and bugles performed a mass reveille, including Colonel Bogey.

The band as usual had to provide the music for the morning service which included the traditional carols. All went as per Order of Service until it came to *The Holly and the Ivy*. The bandmaster forgot to include the chorus in his count and suddenly stopped the band while the congregation sang on, albeit at half volume as they were not certain whether or not they should be singing at all. The BM then tried to start in the right place, but this caused even more chaos. The CO was not happy...

At lunch time the band started a tour of the battalion's dining rooms, Officers' and Sergeants' Messes. Half way through, the bandmaster said to me, 'Carry on with the tour, Corporal, as we (the BM and the sergeants) have been invited to the Officers' Mess for drinks.'

This came as a bit of a shock to me but I think I acquitted my duty without too many gaffs, although there was some leg-pulling afterwards as the pieces I chose to conduct were fairly easy (therefore obviously easy for a 'novice' to conduct.)

It was shortly after this that I found myself was standing in the Orderly Room corridor, for what purpose I can't recall, when the BM came out of one of the doors. Seeing me, he came across and spoke quite excitedly. 'We're off to Kenya fairly soon, Corporal!'

I must have shown my dismay, as he added quickly, 'At least it will mean another medal!'

The battalion underwent another change of Commanding Officer The new CO was as different again from his predecessor as he could have been. He was very much a hands-on man but unfortunately his time with the battalion was destined to be cut short. He was accidentally killed by one of the Bren-gunners while in the forest around the Aberdares in Kenya.

Exactly two years to the day after it had a arrived, the battalion left Gottingen for the U K. On reaching the Hook of Holland we entered into the world of 'Hurry up and Wait' that seems so beloved of the services. Some of the band boys started to play cricket using a kit bag as the stumps and a wooden paling for a bat. They were really enjoying themselves as were a number of the battalion who were watching and calling out in encouragement, when in to view came two L/corporals of the Military Police who immediately got 'heavy' with the boys. I asked what was the problem.

'They should act like soldiers,' I was told.

I pointed out that they were boys and doing no harm. I also said they were better occupying their time than getting into real mischief. 'So why not leave them alone?'

The two MPs departed to many catcalls from those who had been watching. They hovered around some distance away but didn't interfere again.

The battalion returned to Whittington Barracks but while the men occupied the barrack blocks, the boys took over a small house on the perimeter of the barracks. As we entered the building, the one boy who never seemed to engage brain before speaking, piped up. 'Those windows don't look to clean,

Corporal.'

'Fetch your cleaning gear and get cracking, then!' I replied.

He went of to carry out his task and some time later found me to report he had finished, but added, 'They seem rather dirty on the outside.'

'Off you go, then,' I said, and he returned to the task.

The boy returned some time later for me to inspect his work. During my inspection he said. 'These window sills look rather gritty.'

I said nothing, but just looked.

Away he went, and until the day I left the band, although he was now a bandsman, he still opened his mouth before engaging brain!

CHAPTER FOURTEEN

Boots, boots, boots, marching over Africa (Kipling)

Before we left for Africa, we were granted the usual embarkation leave. I went off to spend it with Digs at her parents new house in Eastbourne. It was pleasant change to wear civilian clothes and absorb the seaside atmosphere in a relaxed mood, at least for most of my leave. It was near the end of the school holidays and Digs had to return to her new school in West Norwood The head was good person but I doubt if she would have appreciated the new member of her staff taking more time off than the holidays permitted.

My leave came to an end and I returned to Lichfield to carry out the preparations necessary for the move to East Africa. However, it seemed I was destined, for the time being, to take another path, as one day I went down with a mysterious lower stomach bug and was transported to the Military Hospital in Chester.

As I was not a bed patient, I was granted a day pass for the purpose of seeing the battalion away from , you guessed it, Prince's Dock, Liverpool. I travelled with a lieutenant who was also a patient. I was able to see most of the band, also to have a posed picture taken for the Shrewsbury paper (*The Express and Star*). The lieutenant and I left just before the ship sailed, even so, we were late reporting back to our hospital wards. I made my way down the main corridor of the 'spider' and for some reason I removed my shoes and continued in my stockinged feet. I was nearly in the ward when I heard a voice behind me. 'There's no need to creep around, Corporal.'

It was Matron! And in those days Matrons were to be feared!

As I had arrived back late but, more importantly, got caught, there were questions to be asked and answered, though, when I stated I was in company with an officer there were fewer questions.

I was subjected to various tests but nothing of significance was found and I was discharged back to the Regimental Depot. At the Depot at this time there were men awaiting discharge, undergoing training, and waiting to be posted to the battalion. Amongst the recruits was the son of a local farmer who was in the middle of harvesting and would pay men to work in the evenings (half-past five in the evening until sunset) the princely sum of ten shillings (50p). I can assure you, it was hard work lifting and loading the bales of hay but like most things there was a knack and once you mastered that you really 'earned your corn'. And the farmer's wife made sure we were well fed and watered. I doubt if I've ever been fitter, before or since.

I was warned I was on the list of those due to join the battalion, thus entitled to embarkation leave which I was to start the next day. I said not a word but really enjoyed the next fourteen days and said a prayer to the absent minded clerk who must have forgotten to enter the details of my last 'embarkation' leave ;on my documents.

When I returned from leave I was told that I would be in charge of the next draft, therefore responsible for their safe arrival and their documents at the battalion. The draft assembled. I received the relevant paper work and was instructed to travel by train and London Underground and to report in at the Goodge Street Deep Shelter Transit Facility. On arrival and having seen the draft fed and watered, I decided to make my way home, so in the interests of safety, I asked one of the senior permanent staff where I might deposit the documents securely.

'They're your responsibility, chum,' I was told.

I gave the matter a few minutes thought and, as I wanted to get home and back before the gates of the facility were closed at midnight, decided to 'hide' the envelope in the most obvious place, under my mattress, working on the assumption that nobody would be daft enough to leave them there. I was relieved to find them still there when I got back.

After breakfast the next morning I was instructed to assemble the draft then get aboard a waiting coach to be transported to Blackbushe Airfield in deepest Surrey. Most of the draft were quite excited as this would be the first time they'd left the country, let alone flown in an aircraft. Amongst the passengers was a brigadier who seemed none too happy at having to travel with those of lesser rank and was to prove a little annoying later.

Trooping by air in those early days was very different to the flights of today. The cabin attendants were not quite sure how to act towards the common soldiery but on the other hand did not shirk in their duties and provided plenty of sweets and drinks (soft!). Meals didn't exist, although it wasn't long before air trooping became civilised, and meals were provided on long to medium flights.

We landed at the airfield of El Adem, near Tobtuk in Libya. While the aircraft was refuelling, we obtained a meal and refreshed ourselves. As the heat was really oppressive, I instructed the draft to adopt Shirt Sleeve Order. This meant removing their battle dress blouses and braces, replacing their web belts around their waist, and either rolling or folding their shirt sleeves to above their elbows. They also removed their ties. I had just finished my instructions to the draft in how to do what I had ordered when the brigadier appeared in neatly pressed tan tropical uniform and asked me where the men's tropical uniforms were.

'In their kit bags in the aircraft hold, sir,' I replied.

'Why?' he asked.

'I don't know and as I did not supervise their packing, I can only assume so, sir.'

The brigadier went away muttering something about necessary instructions in future! He was not happy at the answers but there was nothing he could do at that time. We reboarded the aircraft and continued to Nairobi where we were only too pleased to disembark – since leaving El Adem, the plane's interior had been very hot and stuffy. There was no air conditioning in aircraft in those days but if half the articles you read about the re-circulating of bugs these days I wonder if this was no bad thing?

After the usual formalities – Customs and Immigration – we boarded lorries that were to take us no great distance to the battalion main camp at Muthaiga. I say no great distance as Eastleigh Airport could be seen across the valley from our camp.

I handed over the draft and their documents to the Orderly Room Quarter Master Sergeant then, after checking names and numbers, I made my way to the area in which the band and bugles had their living tents pitched. After drawing blankets, sheets, and 'mossie' net, I took over a bed space in the large marquee.

Once I'd made my bed I went for a stroll to familiarise myself with the layout of the camp, or at least that part of it which was of immediate use to me. The camp layout was of the usual format. In the centre was an earth 'square'. Along the main edge were tents containing the offices of the Commanding Officer, the adjutant, the Orderly Room, and Pay Office, across the road from these was the RSM's Office. At ninety degrees on the right was the hut containing the Armoury and, a little further along, the Officers' Mess and tented lines. On the left, facing, was the hut of the Indian Contractor, who ran a barber's shop, a tailor's and, as usual, a shoe making shop. Strange, but no matter where the British Army went in those days, an Indian Contractor always showed up. Just down the road was the NAAFI and Corporals' Bar.

The fourth side was made up of the rifle companies and for some time, tents containing the band of the Rifle Brigade, one of whom of whom was at Kneller Hall the same year as me.

Why we had the pleasure of their company I never knew. However, I did discover, in the short time they were there, some of them used to slip out under the wire at the bottom of the camp during the hours of darkness, then when the men detailed at morning muster to clear up the area outside the fence reached that section of the wire, the absconders would join the fatigue party and gain entry back into the camp. The tented area of Head Quarter Company was by far and away the largest as it contained the band and bugles, the cooks and cook house plus dining tents, MT personnel, and all manner of people who were needed to run a battalion. The guard room was as always situated to cover the main entrance to the camp and in this case was made of corrugated iron sheets with an enclosed exercise area which got really hot during the day and was not a pleasant place to be. During daylight hours it would be staffed by the Regimental Police while at night it would be the base for the guard selected from the companies.

The RSM was still much the same in his misuse of the English language, also in his habit of throwing his arms about. It was this latter behaviour that led to his downfall. During one of his Drill Parades the battalion was paraded by companies and stood shoulder to shoulder facing front. The RSM spotted something, strode across the square with stick in hand., pushed through the front rank and began to harass a soldier in the centre rank in his usual way – that's to say, throwing his arms around like a windmill.

In doing so he struck the soldier. The soldier said and did nothing then, but when the parade was dismissed he made a formal complaint to the adjutant. In a very short space of time the RSM was posted away to be replaced by a new RSM who was the complete opposite. He was clear in his intentions, quiet in his manner but exact in the presentation of his orders. One could say he was almost, but not quite, the double of Rocky, our much-respected former RSM. At last the battalion began to tick and come alive.

One day my presence was requested at the RSM's Office. Full of dread and trepidation I presented myself. The RSM told me to relax as he had glad tidings for me. I was to be promoted with immediate effect to the rank of Local Sergeant. I was very surprised as I'd thought I wouldn't be promoted for a long time yet as, traditionally, promotion in the band was very much a matter of dead men's shoes.

The rank of Local Sergeant is one of those peculiarities that are allowed from time to time when there is no vacancy in a particular rank. It is a supernumerary rank and holds good as long as one remains in the parent unit. Although you hold the substantive rank of Corporal you do enjoy the more comfortable life style of the Sergeants' Mess.

After I had recovered my credulity, the RSM told me to go to the Quarter Master's store and get issued with insignia as befitted my rank. I made my way to the QMS where I exchanged my two chevron brassard for a three chevron one and was also issued with a 5 knot whistle cord, as worn by all from the rank of Sergeant upwards in the Light Infantry. I also drew my red shoulder sash which filled me with a sense of pride impossible to describe every time I wore it.

Because I didn't receive the higher rate of pay, I wasn't asked to pay Sergeants' Mess fees. At the same time, as I no longer frequented the Corporals' Club, I wasn't asked for their fees either! Someone once said that rank has its privileges and I must admit that not having to march to the cookhouse at a set time for one's meals, plus not having to carry one's fighting irons, instead making one's leisurely way to a dining room set out with white table cloths and sitting on individual chairs with each place set with cutlery and glasses of water was indeed a privilege worth having, along with having a 'Boy' to attend to one's laundry and provide one's morning shaving water, plus tea.

Around this time wives and children began to arrive, but owing to the fact that there were no married quarters, most were living in hotels in or near Nairobi, which led to the usual problems, such as late transport or no time to attend to matters in camp (besides Mess functions or dinners). There was a lot of whinging whenever duty kept a man away from his family. The battalion did their best, even to the extent of having built some log cabin type bungalows in the camp perimeter but for some, even these were not good enough, despite the fact they were rent free. One of the senior NCOs was joined by his wife and came up with the idea of living in a caravan. He obtained permission to park his caravan next to the NAAFI, which we all thought rather a strange idea as some of the revelries could be rather noisy, especial on a Friday night. What we didn't know was that he had given the matter much thought and was able to tap not only into the canteen's water supply but also into their electricity and for some time lived quite comfortably at no cost.

But, as I've said, some people are never satisfied and one day a long service NCO in the band was complaining at having to perform some duty or other, saying loud and long, that he had xxx number of children and could not expect his wife to manage on her own!

After a while, having to listen to his perpetual moaning got right under my skin so I turned on him. 'The Army didn't ask you to get married! And no matter how you look at it you're a soldier first. You had your fun having your kids, and I'm sick to death of your moaning.'

I think the message got through as he never, in my hearing, raised the subject again.

I have never understood the stupidity of some people. Once, when a kit inspection was called by the Company Commander, during my preliminary inspection, I discovered that one of the bandsmen had laid out a knife, fork, and spoon. Nothing strange, I hear you say – except that the knife bore the crest of the Governor and the words *Government House*! I managed to maintain a reasonable attitude while asking the man what the blazes he thought he was doing, as not only had he shown he was a thief but also laid the band open to suspicion, especially as we played at Government House so often.

After a few moments' thought I decided to confiscate the knife and return it to Government House with a letter of apology but without naming names. The Company Commander chastised the Bandsman for being deficient of an item of kit. The Bandsman then had to purchase another from the QM store, while I made his life a little more difficult for some time to come.

On my promotion I had to move into a tent in the Sergeants' Mess Lines and I was fortunate enough to share a tent with a Sergeant in the Royal Army Pay Corps attached to the battalion who, like myself, believed in the creature comforts, especially where living accommodation was concerned. One of the first items I obtained was a Safari wash stand, which consisted of a floor standing, wooden cupboard with aluminium bowl complete with plug. The lid has held in place by a catch and had a very good mirror. To use this facility, you first placed a bucket in the cupboard in a position to catch any waste water when you pulled the plug. Everything would be all right, provided you remembered to check the water level in the bucket before use, otherwise wet feet were the order of the day. Many loud curses were heard when the user realised that they were experiencing a wet sensation around the toes!

Another innovation that the majority of the tent occupants engineered was the raising of the tent centre poles on to earth-filled ammunition boxes, thereby giving at least eighteen inches more headroom. We would then obtain a split bamboo which was fashioned into a curtain, then be fixed in position under the raised edge of the roof. This provided a screen but still allowed air to circulate. Whilst on the subject of tents, two things come to mind – one quite humorous, the other not quite so.

The first came about in the perpetual desire of soldiers to plant flowers and place stones around the area between the tent pegs and the side walls of their tents. The men decided to create beds of nasturtiums which climbed the guy ropes and made quite a picture. We didn't have the problems we 'd had in Hong Kong with the tent pegs pulling out in the wet. These ones remained fairly permanent.

One Sunday a Government official was a guest at the Sergeants' Mess for lunch and made the observation that The East African Government was spending thousands of pounds a year to eradicate the 'menace' of the nasturtium, as the plant played havoc in the farming areas! Here were our men cultivating them!

The other not so funny episode concerned sand fleas or, at least, the military solution to them. Sand fleas were fairly harmless although when they bit humans they left a small pink circle with a red dot in the middle. When you made your bed in the mornings it was nothing to find a number of them under your pillow. The powers responsible for our health decided to at least reduce this menace. The way was to lace up every tent and throw a DDT bomb in. Fine, except they forgot to tell us that DDT has an oily base. It took many hours to bring such items as best boots and brasses back up to standard.

As a result of my promotion, I obviously had more and

different duties to perform, one of which was morning muster. During this parade I had to issue Paludrine (anti-malarial tablets) and the recipient had to swallow the tablet in my presence.

Men offered all sorts of excuses as to why they couldn't swallow their tablets. I knew they were trying it on, as I had served with them and knew they were capable of creating a situation, so I decreed that all those who couldn't swallow their tablets without water must bring a mug of water with them when they parade each morning. This led to a debate on the theme, 'How can we keep the water from spilling when we carry out drill movements?'

'You can leave your mugs at the edge of the area until such times as you need them,' I told them. This may seem strange, but I felt a few moments' disturbance to achieve a result was better than letting the fly boys get away with it. The next morning there was not a mug in sight!

Besides band duties, the bandsmen were called upon to perform slightly different tasks, like cutting and collecting bamboo from the forest, to be used in the tents as described. On one of these trips up country we stopped for a couple of nights in a Kenya Police post which was the duty post of an English inspector, an African sergeant and six or seven African constables. We, of course, had brought the unexpired portion of our rations.

The inspector looked at them. 'You didn't need to bring those. Two of my constables are out catching tonight's dinner.'

Some little time later the constables returned to the post

carrying, suspended from the branch of a tree, the carcass of a gazelle. They carried their burden into the office, hung it from one of the beams and departed.

We sat with the inspector, helping him to dispose the best part of a bottle of whisky we'd been advised to bring with us. One of the constables returned and started to skin and gut the carcass We watched, absolutely fascinated, although one or two left the room looking rather green, saying the whisky had got to them. No matter what the effect of the drink, our dinner that night, although the meat was a little rich to our unaccustomed palettes, proved to be excellent.

The next morning we set to our task with a will to get it over and done. The men completed the cutting just before lunch break and one or two were feeling a little boastful so I issued a challenge to one of them.

I would give him a pound (East African) if he could fell an African Blackwood using only the machete he'd been using to cut bamboo. The tree I had chosen was only about eight inches thick, but the African Blackwood is a very hard wood and I had my doubts that he would succeed.

The lad set to with a will and after some time he completed the task. He came to collect his winnings and as I handed over the money I saw that his hands were bleeding quite heavily. I told him, and another man as escort, to return to the Police Post and get his hands dressed. On reflection I should not have issued the challenge as I could have been responsible for him being unable to carry out his duties.

A P Sisley

The Royal Air Force base across the valley requested that the band parade to accompany the Air Officer Commanding's parade, which was held every month or so. We paraded as requested and were absolutely amazed at the state of dress of the airmen concerned. Some were wearing shorts and shoes with knee length socks, while others wore trousers and jackets, or shorts and boots plus long jackets. As for marching, they took some time to get used to what was required but with a little encouragement from the Station Warrant Officer they got the hang of it. A few months later we heard that the airmen had gone on strike, over the food they were getting and their living conditions. To say the least we were flabbergasted! To our eyes, they were living in well equipped barrack blocks with up-to-date eating accommodation while we were living under canvas and, when not eating dust, were ankle deep in murram mud. They got little sympathy from the lads.

After ninety days on the strength of an operational unit one was entitled to wear the ribbon, which, for those who already had some medals was no big thing, but for those with only this ribbon, it was rather a pretty sight. However this was to change rather rapidly, for when Princess Margaret was to pay a visit to the colony and the band was scheduled to play no small part in the activities, we were amazed at the speed with which our medals arrived. (I think the issue must have been done in great haste as my AGSM was inscribed as my serving in the ASLI – which will make a rare collector's piece!

The first engagement connected with the Royal visit was for a Royal garden party in the grounds of Government House.

A SHROPSHIRE BOY

It seems the Governor decided that it would be a good thing to hold a Garden Party as this would give a great number of people the opportunity to see the Royal visitor, although we noticed that most of the people invited were white or Asian, with a sprinkling of African chiefs and elders. Part of our appearance was the usual military band programme. After the Royal walk about, during which HRH was accompanied by two of her equerries (a couple of Ruperts from the King's Royal Rifles), the band and bugles performed the *Sounding of Retreat*. There was nothing strange about this except we performed a new marching display and everybody concerned was keeping their fingers crossed, hoping it would be done correctly. The band were wearing their No 3 Dress (whites), while the buglers wore their No 1 Dress (green). At the start of the display the band stepped off in slow time while the buglers stepped off in quick time. As could have been predicted, a gap soon opened up between the two sections. At the end of the ground to be covered the buglers would counter march and return towards and through the band. At a given point while the two section passed through, a Double Tap would be given on the bass drum and the band would change to quick time, while the buglers changed slow time. This manoeuvre would be carried out a number of times until were moving in the same direction and in the same time.

Our display was greeted with much applause and as we discovered later, the contrast of pace and colour helped to enhance the performance. In the evening we had to play during an official dinner held at Government House. During this program I was to play the tubular bells for the first time, other than in the practice tent. Since abandoning the saxophone, I had for some time been thinking about taking up a second instrument and one day realised that in a dust-covered box lay the answer. I knew my choice would not be popular with those who had to load and unload the instruments, but I started to practice nonetheless and reached a fairly moderate standard in a short space of time, hence my performance this night.

When we thought we had reached the end of our night's work, one of the Ruperts appeared in the door looking very resplendent in his Mess Dress. 'Her Royal Highness has enjoyed your programme very much,' he said. 'Could you play for some dancing when the dinner is over?'

This rather set everyone back, as we had neither the music nor some of the instruments required for dance work. However being the good natured fellow he was the bandmaster said that given the time to despatch one of the lorries back to our camp to collect the music and so on, we would be happy to comply with HRH's request. The dance band were out very late, until the early hours and were very weary when they paraded the next morning.

Our engagements took us far and wide and even into Tanganyika. I forget the exact reason for our visit but I do remember three of us being billeted in the house of the manager of a local canning factory in Arusha, at the foot of Mount Kilimanjaro.He had served in the mountain batteries of the Royal Artillery during the Second World War, and we spent many hours answering questions about home. The mountain, with the moon rising behind it, really is a wonderfully romantic sight – at least, so one of our more amorous members told me (or, rather, his female companion told him!)

Some of the band thought they might make a good walk of this mountain. They were persuaded not to attempt it by some of the people who lived in Arusha. Despite being fairly fit, they really needed knowledge and training before making the ascent. We knew there had been many successful walks in the past years but we bowed to greater experience.

Our second visit to Tanganyika was to the town of Moshi, to perform for the local Brits, most of whom were connected with the Police Training barracks situated on the edge of the town. We were entertained very well indeed but for some reason or other it was decided by the bugle major, another sergeant, the band sergeant and myself not to stay there, but to travel back to our barracks, which was how the four of us came to be speeding through the night across East Africa in the bugle major's car.

The roads in that part of the world had been scraped flat, giving them a very dusty surface which flew up and obscured everything behind. As we had partaken of the hospitality offered we all had rather full bladders and requested the bugle major to stop, which he firmly refused to do. 'If you want to wee, do it in your shoes and toss it out of the window.'

We had no option but to fall in with his idea. We filled a shoe, opened the window and emptied it. This was not the end of the saga, for the road dust was flying and as we emptied our shoes, the sides and the boot became thickly coated with a beautiful red ochre which took the bugle major quite a considerable time to remove.

It was during this nocturnal trip we saw a big, mangy lion, sitting in the middle of the road. When he appeared in the headlights the only thing we could do was stop as there were ditches either side of the carriage way and had we attempted to go around the beast, we would have grounded on the margin of the road. We sat there watching his Lordship scratch and preen himself. Although occasionally he would stretch, he made no attempt to move out of the road. I have to say I've seen lions in better condition in zoos and circuses in England. The specimen in front of us was a flea-bitten, scruffy specimen and I wondered if he survived for long after our encounter. After what seemed a long time he rose and wandered stiffly off into the bush, as though we had never existed. At least we could continue on our way.

One of the most interesting events, as far as I was concerned, was the occasion when the band and bugles performed at a tribal gathering in the Masai Mara.

The Masai Mara was a very much restricted area and to enter you had to obtain permission from a high level, so we thought ourselves honoured to be invited to enter the area.

The reason for our visit was twofold. One was to show the flag; the other to show we still had an interest in the life and ways of the tribesmen. The reason behind the gathering was an inter-village football match. The term 'football' is used loosely as the form it took was far removed from our matches. While we were performing our marches and counter marches the contestants were gathering at each end of the arena, and a frightening lot they looked. When we finished our performance we left the arena but we noticed that the tribesmen had gathered behind the lines at either end of the pitch.

At the appointed time a whistle was blown and a gentleman, who was, I believe, the District Commissioner, stood and threw a football in to the centre of the arena. This was the signal for the two groups of tribesmen to rush towards the centre and each other. They met with considerable force and I still maintain this was more a contest of strength than a football match; the winning team appeared to be the one with the most standing at the end of an allotted time.

We wandered about gazing at the various headdresses of the warriors, especially those made from lions' manes, as this meant the wearer was of certain standing in his tribe, particularly if he had killed the lion himself to obtain the mane. However, we did learn to keep on the move, otherwise we could have found ourselves surrounded by a group of leaping tribesmen which could be rather frightening the first couple of times. I came to admire their standing jumps which I am sure would be the envy of many players in a rugby line-out.

On one occasion we paraded with the band of the Middle East Air Force who had been flown down specially to attend the Kenya Agricultural Show in Nairobi. This didn't worry us too much as the Air Force band were to be the 'House' band, which gave us some free time to roam about and take in all the stalls and attractions. Over the entrance to the main arena was a rather imposing fort-like construction but manning the ramparts, instead of soldiers, there were Masai warriors, covered from head to toe in red murram as is the way of the Masai. They stood in turn for about an hour, after which they were free to wander as we were. During one of their break periods two of our bandsmen and two Masai came face to face.

'Jambo ('Good morning' in Swahili) John,' piped one of our bandsmen.

'Good day to you,' replied one of the warriors. This took the bandsmen back a pace or two but they didn't allow it to prevent an enquiry on their part. It turned out that the two warriors, although true members of the Masai, were undergraduates of Oxford University, earning some spending money while on holiday at home – which just goes to show, you never can be too careful.

During the show, there was a display of agility by four helicopters who had been working up country with the security forces. The four aircraft started their display hovering with their noses facing each other over the centre of the arena. They dipped, then moved backwards into the corners before flying out over the corner stands and coming back into the arena from a new direction. The use of helicopters was still in its infancy and they received tumultuous applause.

CHAPTER FIFTEEN

Drinking is a soldier's game

I have already mentioned the social side of the Sergeants' Mess, and their relationship with other messes, but this relationship wasn't always sweetness and light.

One evening, the RAF Mess invited some of us to a Mess Supper. During the evening a fair amount of beverages were consumed, which prompted two of our number to entertain those present with their interpretation of the Sand Dance. For this they dressed either in table cloths or sheets and lamp shades The climax of their performance was reached when the two of them hurled themselves backwards through an open window. The whole business had required a careful recce outside to ensure that there was nothing upon which they might injure themselves, also that the window was open. The pair went through their routine and launched themselves at the window. Out they went, taking the window frame and all, landing in the garden covered in glass, wood, and putty. It transpired that the window had been refurbished only that morning and the window was closed because earlier in the evening, one of the wives had felt a draught and shut it. There appeared in the space where the window used to be two battered but very happy faces. It was some time before we were invited again.

One of our trips up country took us to Fort Hall where the Chief had acquired a certain standing with the settlers and farmers by nailing the Union Jack to a flag pole and saying loud and long that if the Mau Mau wanted to take the flag down it would be over his dead body!

We travelled in three 3-ton lorries and a 1-ton vehicle, driven this time by African drivers of the Royal Army Service Corps. We started on the way back with the 1-tonner in the lead, carrying the bandmaster in the front and me in the back. The 3-tonner trailed along behind. The road, although murram, had a good surface At one point the road went down an incline, turned left over a narrow bridge with a low parapet.

The 1-tonner negotiated the bend and the bridge all right, but the 3-tonner descended the slope a little too fast, attempted to turn on to the bridge, hit the parapet, leapt into the air and descended into the river beneath. Luckily the river was high and only three feet or so beneath the parapet, and the lorry hit the water flat, maintained buoyancy and stayed upright. I saw what happened and shouted for the BM to stop.

When our truck stopped I jumped out and dashed down into the hip high water and started to check the men. It turned out that although there were one or two minor cuts and grazes, most were able to assist in unloading the instruments and kit, while the bandmaster stood on the bank shouting. 'Mind the instruments!! Mind the instruments!'

The comments he received in reply could have led to charges if he had been of such a mind but we got away with it. It so happened that a lorry carrying some of those we had been playing to earlier came along and offered to take the injured, plus me, to a mission about three miles away, where they were sure we could get help and the use of a telephone.

At the mission, we dismounted but foolishly, after thanking them, sent our rescuers on their way before I was able to attract the attention of the occupants of the mission, who seemed very reluctant to answer our knocking. Eventually a priest spoke to me through a grille in the gate but despite our pleas for at least a sticking plaster, refused to have anything to do with us. Maybe he was frightened the Mau Mau might hear that they had helped us.

We sat in the shade wondering what to do next when a lorry on its way to Fort Hall spotted us and stopped. We boarded the lorry and were transported back to the bridge to rejoin the members of the band awaiting transport back to Muthaga.

In camp one of the main problems was dust! This could never be entirely dealt with but for all that it didn't stop the Company Commander from striding through the tents, beating the stretched blankets on all the beds with his swagger cane and shouting: 'Dust!'

We tried every way to get around this, from shaking the blankets at the very last minute before inspection to sprinkling water around the tent floor, but we never escaped the swagger cane strike and the cry, 'Dust!'

However, life wasn't all one-sided, as occasionally something would occur that made things a little more bearable. Someone, somewhere had the marvellous idea that it would not only be easier but also smarter if the battalion wore stable belts when not on official parades. The belt was of woven material and bore the regimental colours: scarlet over old gold over royal blue over LI green, fastened by two small leather straps. Another brilliant idea was to replace the wearing of gaiters with short puttees and hose tops of LI green The thing to remember in the wearing of puttees was to end with the upright seam just in front of the ankle bone, which meant the surplus of the fastening tape would be wound around the binding tape behind the ankle bone. This may sound a fiddly business but it was better than having to blanco one's gaiters, and black the straps and polish the buckles. With practice you could get these puttees on in a matter of minutes.

As a 'married (unaccompanied)', it transpired that I was entitled to home leave every nine months. (I wonder who fixed that particular period?) and in due course I was granted this leave. I reported to the local transit camp and was checked in for a flight home. We were informed that after take off from Nairobi we would be flying only as far as Entebbe, since the plane couldn't take off from Nairobi with full fuel tanks. We didn't have the travel knowledge that is available today and didn't realise that the airstrip was the problem. It seems it was just not long enough, despite being in use by the RAF. We landed at Entebbe and, after refuelling, carried on to Malta. Amongst the passengers was a family flying home on transfer and in their number a very small boy who had never seen the sea close up before so it fell to his father to attempt an explanation, while the youngster stood gazing out to sea. When we restarted our journey the child was still quizzing his father. (Oh for the innocence of childhood!)

The remainder of the journey was uneventful and after landing at Blackbushe and passing through Customs we went our separate ways. I knew Digs was on the Isle of Wight with a school party so decided to go direct to Shanklin rather than to the flat then make another journey. It was while crossing on the ferry that I got into conversation with the Drum Major of the Women's Royal Air Force band and a very interesting person she was. My time spent with the children went all too quickly but they were great fun and great company and I was sad when the time came for us to return to London.

On our return to the flat, I found an official letter awaiting my return. It transpired that between my arrival on the Isle of Wight and my return to the flat, the Deep Shelter in Goodge Street had suffered a major fire therefore no further troop movements through this particular place were possible. I was instructed to remain at my given address until further notice. The inevitable question of money arose but I need not have been concerned as a few days later communication arrived containing pay and ration allowance for the next twenty-one days, plus a questionnaire asking where my unit was stationed and by which mode of transport I might like to return: boat or plane? Naturally, I chose the sea, thinking a nice leisurely sea cruise might suit me, especially as the political climate at that time might mean a trip around Cape Horn to avoid Suez. I heard nothing for nearly three weeks which was well past my original date of return.

To fill in some of the time while Digs was at work I pursued my hobby of medal collecting, which meant visiting various dealers in central London.

On one occasion I wore uniform and as I ascended the escalator into the booking hall at one of London's main stations, I saw to my amazement two figures in uniform wearing the flashes of the KSLI. They were both leaning up against a wall, smoking. Their berets were tucked underneath their epaulettes, and they had removed their waist belts. They had not seen me so I crept round behind them.

'What the hell do you think you're doing?' I barked.

To say they were taken aback would be an understatement.

I first instructed them in a very low voice to put out their cigarettes and dispose of the butts in a nearby bin. I then instructed them to replace their berets and waist belts, in other words, get themselves properly dressed and then stand to attention in front of me. I asked them to inform me exactly what their were doing in the centre of London. It appeared they were in transit via Woolwich to join the battalion. I gave them some advice regarding their future conduct, and told them I would see them upon my return to Kenya so they didn't get any ideas that this matter was over. They had behaved in a manner that was not in keeping with regimental expectations. I sent them on their way and suddenly realised I had not raised my voice above a normal speaking volume throughout this encounter, which might have given rise to one of the ticket collectors saying, as I passed, 'Nicely done, Sarge.'

Notice for my return duly arrived, stating I was to report to the transit facility in the Royal Artillery Depot, Woolwich, for onward passage to Nairobi *by air*.

I reported in at a reasonable time, as Woolwich was not too far from the flat and I even thought I might get another night at home before leaving these shores once again. I was instructed to obtain a bed space in the designated barrack room and promptly did so I immediately asked the men already in transit what the procedure was. Some of those waiting had been there some days and it seemed to be 'luck of the draw' when the roll was called at nine o'clock in the morning. I decided that nine o'clock would suit me fine, so without further ado I took myself out through the barracks gates, boarded a bus from a stop just outside and within thirty five minutes deposited myself on a settee in the front room of the flat. After a peaceful night I returned to Woolwich in time for morning muster and sure enough my name was on the list of those flying out that day. (I later found out that my return had been especially requested.)

Those chosen that day were transported to Blackbushe where we went through the routine that was becoming fairly familiar before boarding the plane, which was destined to take the route via El Adem. When at last, we took off from the desert airfield, the plane was full of hot, humid air which meant we had a fairly uncomfortable last leg to Nairobi.

On rejoining the band it took no time to get back into the routines although these were to be disrupted by the battalion's rather fast move to the Persian Gulf to take up defensive positions covering the oil fields because of the Suez crisis.

The Band were left behind, along with men awaiting demob, to guard the camp and carry out other duties as required. We carried on with practice as usual, although 'as required' raised its head and we were engaged in such tasks as striking the tents left by the rifle companies. We had some doubts as to the wisdom of this, since we felt the battalion would not be away too long and would require these tents on their return, along with the bamboo 'curtains' which, although simple enough, took time to make.

Extra duties fell upon the senior NCOs in that they were

required to carry out the duties of Orderly Sergeant and Guard Commander. In the performance of these duties common sense seems to have prevailed The Orderly Sergeant took up his duties at 09:00 hrs and carried right through to 09:00 hrs the next morning. The Sergeant would carry out duties as normal until after Defaulters parade at 23:00, when he would take over the duties of Guard Commander from the Corporal of the Guard. This may seem a little strange but we found it worked, especially if the corporal was co-operative in taking a share of the duties and allowed one to get a few cat naps in. The system also meant that duties did not come around quite so often.

Things sometimes went a little awry and one such occasion comes to mind very clearly. I was Orderly Sergeant and it was part of my duties to carry out Guard Mount in company with the Orderly Officer, (who had not long been out from Sandhurst). The Guard formed up on the parade ground in the following order. The Guard Commander took his position on the right hand of the front rank with the Bugler on his left hand but between the Commander and the Guard. On the command 'Guard Commander and Bugler', both would come to attention. The Guard Commander would shoulder his arms and both would advance fifteen paces and halt. The Guard Commander would order arms then both he and the Bugler would stand at ease. On this occasion only the Bugler moved. I uttered the usual words about 'waking up', and gave the order again. Once again only the Bugler moved. I advanced towards the Guard. 'Don't you know what to do, Corporal?' I asked.

He replied that he had only returned to the battalion two

280

days before to await demob. I said, 'Did it not occur to you on seeing your name posted for duty to spend a few minutes finding out what you are supposed to do?'

I realised I was going to get nowhere so did a quick think and asked the lance-corporal if he knew what to do. He replied he did, so I ordered them to change places. The Guard Mount got under way again without a hitch until I reported, 'Guard ready for inspection, Sir,' when to my surprise the Orderly Officer said, 'What do I do now, Sergeant?'

I said I would give the relevant commands and he should pick up the routine from these. The next hitch came when the Orderly Officer had to inspect the rifles of the Guard. Under normal mount conditions, the Guard Commander is by tradition exempt from this inspection but here we had a different situation and to my mind the 'deposed' Guard Commander had forfeited this privilege and the l/corporal was now in the position of exemption. The Orderly Officer was not of a like mind so I had to steer him a little. The end result was the corporal had his rifle inspected and was found to have a dirty barrel, for which he was reported. (He got away without punishment as he flew out a couple of days later.)

When the battalion had departed those in authority decided that to add strength to the camp's guard, guard dogs would be placed around the perimeter. The dogs were attached by their collar chains to running wires which were firmly pegged into the ground at certain strategic points. The men carrying out prowler sentry duties during the hours of darkness had to remember exactly where the dogs were as they were not too particular into whom they sank their fangs! The dogs were kennelled during the day in an area just behind the Guard Room and we often saw them undergoing training. The handlers would tease them with large pieces of raw meat and like humans who had been awake most of the previous night the dogs were not in a playful mood. Some of the handlers had some very near misses. I often thought heaven help anyone getting too near the dogs none-too-clean fangs.

The Band went *en masse* to spend their local leave at the Silver Sands leave centre in Mombasa. The only exceptions being myself and one other of the Senior NCOs. I couldn't go because I had been on leave in the UK, while the other had arranged to spend his leave travelling around Lake Victoria on one of the steamers that plied their trade there. On his return he said he wouldn't have missed the experience for the world.

I think he must have become sympathetic towards Africa and the Africans as he eventually joined our former bandmaster in the Rhodesian Police. As for me, I was left in camp with one or two duties to carry out. One of these required me to take the Band's No. 1 Dress uniforms to be dry cleaned at a laundry situated on the edge of the forest, some ten miles from the camp. During this trip the idea came to me that as I had qualified as a War Emergency driver it might provide an ideal opportunity to hone my skills. I decided to go legal and asked the permission of the officer left in command who also happened to be the battalion Motor Transport Officer. I asked if he could grant me a few minutes of his precious time. When I put my idea to him he refused point blank. 'The battalion transport is not a plaything for the gratification of your ideas!'

I wasn't too disappointed as I had already made an agreement with the driver that when we started away from the main road I would take over the wheel, which I did and spent some time driving around. It was quite amazing the number of times there was a pair of trousers or tunic missing or some that needed more attention, requiring me to go and have words with the contractor. My driving skills certainly improved.

While on the subject of driving.... one of the sergeants in the Band, who, as a Boy, was the lad with whom I'd had the boxing match in the gym in Shrewsbury, had grown much bigger and taller and had bought himself a Ford Popular car. Such was the size of the chap that when driving his car, if he wanted to turn left, he would wind down the passenger window and place his arm through it. This often caused some wonderment among other drivers.

It was around this time, that another incident cropped up. As I mentioned, the duties of the Orderly Sergeant covered twenty four hours and as the Guard dismounted at Reveille, I was already up and about. I decided to call in at the Cook House for a cuppa. On reaching it, I found the place in complete darkness and securely locked. I knew the cook had received an early call because under the system at that time the sentry going through the camp giving early calls had to receive a signature from those affected, so there could be no excuses. I made my way to the tent concerned and enquired who was the duty cook. Upon receiving the relevant information I tipped the offender out of his bed with the warning that if he was not in the cookhouse properly washed shaved and dressed in fifteen minutes he would be looking at the largest amount of 'jankers' the law allowed! I proceeded through the camp checking on various points then decided to check on the wayward one. You can imagine my surprise when on entering the cookhouse kitchen I saw the cook stirring the porridge with a poker! I immediately had words and warned him that if I had any more of his antics, I would place him in close arrest. I realised straight away that this would be a stupid move, for if I carried out my threat, a lot of men would either be late for muster or go without breakfast. I think he got the message as I heard on the grapevine that when I was Orderly Sergeant, I was one to be watched.

An incident occurred when I was Guard Commander on another occasion, when one of the men decided to return to camp drunk. While I was dealing with the matter of admitting him to the camp he collapsed on to the floor of the Guard Room. At this moment the Orderly Officer entered the Guard Room, saw two members of the Guard trying to bring the man back to a state where they could get him back to his tent.

'This man is ill!' said our recent arrival from Sandhurst.

I assured him the man was under the influence, as such, a candidate for a night in the cells.

'I beg to differ,' said the Rupert, 'and I want the duty driver turned out and this man taken to BMH.'

I had no option but to comply as our MO was with the

battalion in Bahrain. The duty driver was summoned and the man duly dispatched. The driver returned about an hour later but offered no new information, so I thought the matter was closed.

How wrong could I be?

About three in the morning, an ambulance arrived at the gate and deposited our wayward lad, who was either a very good actor or still under the influence. The ambulance driver handed me the sick report I had written some hours before.

Across the form in bright red ink someone else had written, 'Please refrain from wasting our time. THIS MAN IS DRUNK.'

The man himself was making quite a noise so in an attempt not to disturb the others of the Guard and the camp, I decided to place him in one of the cells.

Wrong! The Guard Room was built of corrugated iron sheets and as soon as the cell door was shut the drunk started to rattle the walls with a mug one of the Guard had given him, containing water because he said he felt thirsty. I wasn't happy when I found out. I removed the mug but this had no effect and he beat the walls with his stockinged feet. I requested that he stop making a noise and received in return a mouthful of abuse, as well as a statement doubting my parentage. A couple of the Guard asked if there was any way to stop the noise as they were trying to get some sleep during their period off sentry.

In the end, I picked up a rifle and threw open the cell door. 'If you don't stop making a noise, I will wrap this rifle round your ears!'

At this point, I heard a voice behind me. 'You can't do that, Sergeant.'

It was the Rupert, who must have come into the Guard Room just as I entered the cells. I wondered what he was doing out of his bed at that hour of the night. I assured him I would take any measures necessary to ensure the members of the Guard got what rest they could. The drunk seemed to enjoy our difference of opinion, sank to the floor and went to sleep! The Rupert said he would be having words with the Camp Commander in the morning.

I handed over the inscribed sick report and said I hoped he would be taking it with him when he saw the Commander.

Just before hand-over in the morning I was called to attend the camp commander's office. As I approached his tent I saw the Rupert leaving in rather a hurry. I made my presence known and was instructed to enter. The Camp Commander leaned back in his chair. 'I've spoken to the officer concerned in the encounter last night and while I realise he has a lot to learn, I advised him that the best way to learn is to listen to the Senior NCOs and not be afraid to ask their advice. With regard to your threat to wrap a rifle round someone's ears, that might be a little drastic and rather messy, although I realise you had the guards' welfare at heart. Thank you, and good morning.'

One night during one of my tours of duty as Orderly Sergeant some of the 'Old Soldiers' decided to play up in the 'wet' canteen. They obviously thought, 'He's only a sprog, knows nowt, and would never dare try and control the old 'uns!'

I told them to behave or I would close the beer bar. The first reaction was a load of abuse stating amongst other things that I would never dare close the bar. I ordered the manager to close the bar and after the shutters had been pulled down I left the canteen. An idea came to me that I felt sure would solve the problem looming on the horizon. I made my way to the Sergeant's Mess lines to the tent of a sergeant who kept an Alsatian which I knew to be fairly lively but could be controlled by someone whom he knew. The sergeant also let me have a fairly long running lead. I returned to the wet canteen where there was a lot of boasting going on about how they 'fixed that twit of a Sergeant!'

As I walked into the canteen, I saw that the shutter of the bar had been raised and beer was being sold once more. I sent for the manager and told him to close the bar. I also told him he would be reported to the Camp Commander in the morning; and if he opened the bar again tonight, I would place him in close arrest. (NAAFI personnel abroad are subject to Military Law.)

My attention then turned to those who thought I was an easy touch. I knew the trouble-makers, as they'd been in the battalion for years and had never been any different. The persons concerned were seated around a table in front of one of the windows. (I use the word 'window' loosely, as they were square holes cut into the walls with a wooden shutter which was bolted down at night or just closed if the weather got really inclement; otherwise they would be latched open.)

The miscreants were becoming rather vocal, offering the

opinion that I would never let the dog loose.

'You have twenty seconds,' I replied, 'to leave the canteen. Otherwise I release the dog.'

The usual doubts were expressed while I both counted the time and reached down for the release catch on the running lead. I issued a final warning, but only one man moved past me looking rather apprehensive and somewhat frightened. No other move was made, so I 'released' the dog onto the first catch on the running lead so that he would be checked just short of the offending persons. The dog flew across the floor like a jet and I have never seen people move so fast before or since while throwing themselves out through the windows!

Next morning I made my report to the Camp Commander, the result of which the NAAFI Manager was cautioned regarding his future behaviour and reminded that he was under Military Law and must obey any lawful order or instruction given to him. With regard to the 'Old Soldiers', the camp commander thought they had learned enough lessons for one night.

A SHROPSHIRE BOY

CHAPTER SIXTEEN

Music in my heart I bore (Wordsworth)

The battalion returned from the Persian Gulf and many loud curses echoed around the camp, especially from those whose tents we had dismantled.

Peace returned, but not for long!

Someone decided that all bandsmen would take part in a refresher course on the use of rifles and Sterling sub-machine guns. Why this was decided is beyond me as many of the older ex-Boys had never fired a musketry course and were really not familiar with fire arms.

However, off we went to Kangama Rifle Range where we were greeted by the major who had been involved in the broom stick 'incident' in Shrewsbury. He wasn't particularly pleased to see us, but nevertheless got on with his lecture on the safe handling of fire arms with some strong advice about failing to observe the primary rules – i.e.: placing the safety catch in the 'On' position whenever handling a weapon, as well as ensuring that there were no rounds in a position to be fired under the same conditions.

The major stood slightly down range and in front of the

bandsmen who were standing on the firing point with their left shoulder down range and their rifles held at waist height with the muzzles pointed at the ground. The major had just finished his talk when the sound of a shot being fired rang out and a spurt of dust appeared between his feet!

The major took off skywards but there was nothing he could do as he should have had the weapons checked before placing himself in such a dangerous position down range.

The rifles in service with the battalion at this time were Lee Enfield Mark 5s. The Mark 5 was in most respects the same as previous models, except that they were shorter, had a flash eliminator, and a butt plate of almost two inches of solid rubber. The idea of shortening the rifle came through experiences gained in Malayan jungle fighting conditions.

It was a good weapon, with the drawback that after firing,

the firer got quite a shock from a burn between his thumb and first finger, caused by the lack of wood on the upper part of the barrel. There were many loud curses!

Owing to the Emergency regulations and the ability of members of the Mau Mau to take spent cartridge cases and refurbish them for use in their home made rifles, every spent cartridge case had to be accounted for and on return to camp counted, then handed over to the weapons storeman. I often wondered what would have happened if the count had been incorrect. Would they have sent the men back to the range until the missing cases had been found?

The Mau Mau's home-made rifles usually consisted of a length of metal conduit piping, laid into a shaped piece of wood. The 'firing block' was made of lead with a nail placed in the face as a firing pin. A strip of rubber from an old inner tube was fastened over the loading end of the pipe, the firing block was placed inside the rubber strip. A cartridge was placed inside the pipe and the firer would pull back and release the block as many times as it took to fire the refurbished cartridge. It has been claimed that there was more danger behind these 'rifles' than in front of them, which didn't surprise me.

To count the spent cases on our return to camp, we obtained from the armourer a wooden block in which had been drilled 100 holes, just big enough to take the cases. The system worked well until you lost count of how many times you had emptied the blocks. I hit on an idea and asked the armourer if he had any spare blocks. He looked rather puzzled but handed over three blocks and I set to work. For every block that was filled I took the hundredth case and placed it into the 'spare' block. My system beat any other ideas up until then, and saved a lot of time.

The dance band were very much in demand as by this time most of 49th Brigade had been moved from the colony, leaving us and the Kenya Regiment, plus the King's African Rifles to carry the banner. Whenever we were playing at a dance for other units, you could almost always safely bet on an incident taking place, and not always pleasant. One such incident occurred at the British Military Hospital. It seems one member of the staff accused another soldier of trying to attract the attentions of his girl friend (a member of the nursing staff). Things got very heated and blows were exchanged. One of the contestants fell over backwards and I'll never forget the horrible sound of his head hitting the concrete floor. Despite the fact we were in a hospital, the man died without regaining consciousness.

One day the band joined forces with the bands of the Kenya and Uganda Battalions of the King's African Rifles to rehearse for some occasion or other, which, as far as I can remember, never came about. The African bands had both British and African bandmasters but it was the African bandmaster of the Ugandan band that came to our attention. While waiting for things to get started we got into conversation with our African counterparts, and while we were talking, the African bandmaster came to the conductor's stand and raised his hand for silence. Our stand were a little slow in reacting and he just stared at us. The Africans were looking rather scared and one whispered, 'George is a witch doctor. He can do many things of magic!'

George kept looking in our direction and suddenly there was a gust of wind and our music was lifted from our stand and landed about five yards away! Ours was the only stand affected.

To this day I still wonder if it was witch doctor's magic. At the time, I could find no logical explanation for it.

Our bandmaster was asked by the Nairobi Amateur Operatic Society asking if any of the band could help with the orchestra for their production of *The Pirates of Penzance*. They needed a trumpet, a clarinet and a string bass. The BM suggested I might like to go along and help out with the bass. I went along and despite not being very proficient with the bow was welcomed most warmly. The cast were really enthusiastic, in fact the man who played the part of the Major General had spent a great part of his last home leave watching and listening to the D'Oyly Carte Opera Company from the wings of the theatre in London and it showed in his performance. He really was brilliant. I enjoyed the experience immensely and have always been thankful for this opportunity. The production was first class and really gave me a liking for all Gilbert and Sullivan works.

Through the vibrant social life of the Sergeants' Mess I was lucky enough to become friends with an English family who lived in Nairobi, which led to invitations to join them at many events within their social circle. This unfortunately also led to comments among the band regarding my private life, but I was able to squash them before they became too deeply entrenched.

One evening on Daily Orders I read I was to parade for CO's Orders the next morning. My mind was in turmoil trying to fathom out why. When the call sounded the next day I paraded, dressed in my best, well starched shirt and Ghurka shorts and highly bulled boots. I need not have worried for, after being marched in front of the CO, I was informed that the Light Infantry were looking for an NCO to take on the work of training Boys at Strensall (the depot of The King's Own Yorkshire LI). My name was being put forward for the post as the CO thought that since I'd been 'through the mill' as a boy, I would do a good job. To say I was bewildered isn't strong enough to describe my thoughts at the time. I was absolutely astounded that anyone should think I was proficient enough even to be considered.

Around this time a BBC Television crew appeared to make a short film to be included in a programme that would be broadcast at home around Christmas time. One must remember that television was still a new toy at this stage, so Digs, her mother and father had to go to a nearby pub, where there was a television in the lounge. The programme was shown but unfortunately the way the shot had been framed it showed only the bottom half of those standing on the forms at the back, and I was one of those at the back!

The band and bugles were invited to assist in making a record which was then sold in aid of the Kenyan Olympic team going to compete in the Rome Olympics in 1960. The main theme on the record was 'Kenya, Land of the Lion', a song composed by a local musician and arranged for military band by our own BM. The recording took place in Nairobi Cathedral and should have been sung by the Cathedral choir but when the time came to start, few of the choir had turned up. This caused mild panic, until it was suggested that the buglers sang the words. Amazingly, unless they'd been told, anyone purchasing the record would be none the wiser. Just before he died two years ago one of the band who'd also played in the session gave me a tape of the recording. I still play it occasionally, just for old time's sake and I must admit the finished product really wasn't bad.

This same bandsman had a habit I hadn't seen before, nor since. After a heavy session in the canteen he would make his way back to his tent, fall flat on his face on his bed, always placing one hand on the floor, and there he would stay until the next morning. I once asked him about this practice, and he told me that as long as he kept in contact with the floor he was neither sick, poorly nor hung over – and it worked.

As Christmas was coming along some of us decided to go round the suburbs of Nairobi and play carols and Christmas songs in a bid to raise money in aid of work being done on the Regimental Chapel in St Chad's Church, Shrewsbury. I forget the exact combination of instruments but seem to remember euphonium, cornets, clarinets, and alto saxophone. We played outside several apartment blocks, making a very seasonal sound. While the others played, a colleague and I were given the task of knocking on doors. Most respondents seemed to enjoy the efforts and gave very generously, though on at least three occasions, the occupant answered the door wrapped in a towel, as we seemed to have caught them in the shower.

During our tour we took in various Officers' and Sergeants' Messes When we arrived at the Brigade Head Quarters Officers' Mess, they were just about to leave the table having had a Guest night. We played most of our Carols, and they too proved most generous.

Being the festive season, the dance band was much in demand and it was after one of our performances that the '3-tonner curse' hit again. After the dance we went to look for our transport. We had travelled to the venue in the 3-tonner and a 15cwt truck. We could find the driver of the smaller lorry, but there was no sign of the other driver. One of the other NCOs was left to chase up the wayward driver while I went back in the available truck. Later that night I was told that the 3-tonner had been involved in an accident and there were casualties, who had been taken to BMH. The next morning the whole story emerged. The driver (European) had been found and, to the NCO, appeared all right, although as the journey went on the driver's competence showed room for doubt. They were almost in sight of the camp when the lorry had to travel down an incline in the road, at the bottom of which it failed to negotiate a bend, left the road and crashed into a gully causing injuries, in one case seriously. One bandsman (Charlie Hinsley) failed to respond to treatment and died on December 24th. This tragedy cast a shadow over all of us, to say the least, and Christmas was not really celebrated to the full. However, this was not the end of the story.

A SHROPSHIRE BOY

One afternoon I was passing one of the large tents used for giving lectures when I heard voices being raised, some of which I recognised. I entered the tent to find all the bandsmen plus two of the l/corporals in a very heated state. I asked what was going on and was informed that those present were not happy about the fact that the BM, whose wife was a patient in the BMH, had not once during his visits been to see the dying bandsman. They also declared they would not perform under his baton unless something was done.

Seeing the mood the lads were in, I could not but sympathise, though I warned them that what they intended could be looked on as mutiny and as they were on active service they all knew the penalty for that. Nevertheless, I did tell them that their grievances would be passed on. They then dispersed and I sought out the Band Colour Sergeant who said he would do what he could.

On the day of our colleague's burial, we paraded on the road leading into the cemetery and played a funeral march, as is the custom. However, custom was then broken, for instead of the pall bearers coming from the band they were supplied by one of the Rifle Companies, as the bandsmen were required to 'play him away'. This was one of the saddest occasions I had ever been part of. We really were losing one of our own.

A handful of earth was taken from the grave and placed in a Light Infantry Green pouch which in turn was placed inside a teak casket lined with same material as used for the pouch.. A plate was engraved with all relevant details then screwed to the lid. All the band signed a card of condolence, which was taken home by one of the band who came from the same town and had finished his time. It was the least we could do. Nothing more was said until the day after we had buried Charlie, when the BM cornered me in his office. 'What would you have done?' he asked.

I gave him a straight reply. 'I would have at least put my head round his door at the hospital.'

I'm sure this wasn't the answer he wanted but I knew the men and this would at least have prevented the near mutiny. About a week after the incident and despite the unwritten law that you never talk shop in the Mess the RSM took me to one and said he had heard what had happened and he agreed with the action I had taken.

'We'll make a senior NCO of you yet,' he said with a smile on his face, then challenged me to a game of darts with the loser paying for the next round of drinks. Needless to say I lost. (You never won when he challenged.)

The annual Paardeberg Ball (commemorating the great Boer War Battle) came round and it turned out that it was my turn for dance band duty. During the evening, the BM spoke to me. 'Isn't this your first Paardeberg?'

I told him it was.

'I'll take over, then,' he said. 'Go and enjoy yourself.'

The Paardeberg Ball was held in February to celebrate both the Battle Honour, and the fact that the Senior NCOs took command of the battalion when all the officers had been either killed or wounded. The Ball was always a very special event and many were they who made pointed comments in the hope of receiving an invitation. I have to admit I indulged rather heavily that night and was quite worried the next morning by what the other occupant of the tent said.

'Do you know who you were chatting up last night?'

I replied I did not and was informed it was the wife of one of the officers in the battalion. Later in the morning the band had to play for a church service and in the congregation was the lady in question. The lady caught my eye and smiled, so I thought, given the opportunity, I would apologise. We were scheduled to play for the Officers' Mess lunch and while I was moving my gear from one venue to the other the lady passed quite close by so I took the chance to tell her I was sorry if I had caused her any embarrassment or distress the previous evening. She replied that I had behaved very politely. 'I rather enjoyed it all. Thank you,' she added.

Was she just being polite?

One day when the band and bugles were rehearsing a movement on the drill square the commanding officer appeared and instructed all those present to remove their head dress. He then proceeded to inspect everyone's hair cut. When he had finished he told the bugle major to fetch the Indian contractor and the camp barber. They both duly appeared and were, like us, rather bewildered as to what it was all about.

When the CO was ready he took the barber around the ranks and every so often the word 'Coconut' was heard, to which the barber replied, 'Me no give coraganut!'

The CO finished his tour and told the contractor that the

barber had better improve his finished product or he would be finished! We all wondered about this sudden interest in our hair cuts until eventually the information got around that a lady whose husband was of some influence had commented how nice it would be for all concerned to see the men with a decent haircut when they had to remove their head dress for a performance. Shortly after this a National Serviceman who had been a hair dresser in civilian life was given permission to open a hair dressing salon in a small tent. He was kept very busy indeed but at least we felt a little more human.

Sundays in the Sergeants' Mess abroad was always something special. The Cook Sergeant would present one of his curry specialities, the sergeants who lived out would come in, very often bringing their wives and friends, so the mess would be a hive of activity. It invariably attracted members of other messes and regiments so we were sometimes given the opportunity to get our own back for pranks that had been played on us during social evenings.

One particular Sergeant from the Kenya Regiment who was not only a livewire, but also a very brave man, was a wonderful person to know, although I for one would not get on the wrong side of him! The Kenya Regiment was affiliated to the King's Royal Rifles and wore a cap badge depicting a water buffalo. It was composed entirely of European and Indian settlers, businessmen and their sons The regiment had a wonderful war record and served with distinction during the Mau Mau Emergency, especially when it came to gathering information about the gangs. It may not be known that in penetrating the gangs, although the Europeans disguised themselves, they could not at that time disguise their eye colour and this could lead to very tricky situations. (What could they have achieved with modern contact lenses?)

When Kenya gained its independence, the regiment was disbanded and the regimental colours were lodged in the regimental chapel of the Light Division, Winchester. Whenever I attended a re-union there I always paid a silent homage to those gallant gentlemen and their wives who stood up to defend their homes and families from a wicked terrorist movement, amongst the most evil in the world.

I enjoyed visits to other messes, but I fear these social events were not without their dangers. If you paid a visit to one particular mess you always made sure you wore a tie of no particular significance, or otherwise, while enjoying their hospitality you would feel a slight tug at the neck, which would be your tie being cut off and on its way to join what seemed to be hundreds of other pieces of neckwear pinned to the rafters.

One of the other dangers concerned transport. Whenever the Mess went out, one of the sergeants would drive and every so often would ask directions and if he received the instruction, 'Straight on at the next roundabout,' that is exactly what he did – straight over the top!

One matter that upset a lot of the troops was an article in the newspapers back home by a female Labour M P. The 49th Independent Brigade, to which we belonged, wore a shoulder patch consisting of two interwoven Ks which caused this labour MP to make the statement in which she called us the 'Kenya Killers'. I am sure if she had taken the trouble to visit Kenya she would have made a very different statement. Who knows, she might even have praised the troops who, after all, were only doing the bidding of their political masters and even saving lives. (The symbolism behind the shoulder patch was that all the regiments in the Brigade had served in both Korea and Kenya.)

The men looked forward with much enthusiasm to the 'educational' visits to the San Miguel brewery, situated about two miles down the road. These visits always seemed to turn into a contest to see how much they could drink and how fast the brewery could produce their product. The brewery had a roof garden where after the boring business of going round watching bottles being filled, the management invited the visitors to relax and help to empty those bottles. Then the contest really got going.

Many were the times one or other of the contestants had to be restrained from his quest to prove he was related to Superman and did not need the stairs to reach the ground level. As the brewery was within walking distance of the camp more often than not the transport was sent back early and we would walk back when ready. I cannot recall anyone getting into trouble upon reaching the camp gate, maybe because such a large number of the battalion made the visit.

Another 'educational' visit was to the National Game Park,

not far from Nairobi. Much amusement was caused by the antics of the baboons there. These creatures thought nothing of stealing the windscreen wipers, bending the wireless aerials into all sorts of shapes and urinating or depositing excreta all over our vehicle. They could cause many hours of extra work for the driver of the minibus as it would almost certainly be required by either the married families, dance band or one of the messes that evening.

While on the subject of recreation and related events, I'm reminded that one afternoon I caught the early transport into Nairobi and went to a cinema. After the show I was walking along the main street on the way to my friends' apartment when an RAF Police Land Rover containing two RAF policemen came alongside. One of them called, 'Hey, soldier!'

I took no notice as it has always been my policy to address members of the Armed Services by their rank and expect the same courtesy wherever possible. I continued walking.

They called out again, and I still ignored them. I could sense their hackles rising but I felt there was room for a lesson to be learned. Eventually one of the corporals left the vehicle and placed himself directly in front of me. With no reference to my rank, he asked, 'Have you been round in the back streets this afternoon?'

I told him I hadn't.

'When did you arrive here?' the corporal asked.

I was getting a little tired of this game so I asked did he mean in Kenya or Nairobi?

'In Nairobi.'

'At two thirty this afternoon.'

'Can you prove this?'

By chance, I had retained the ticket stub which I'd received when I'd booked my seat, which was date and time stamped. I produced the stub but this did not seem to satisfy him and he made some caustic remark. By this time I was getting a little hot under the collar so I asked the corporal what it was that was hanging from my left shoulder.

'A lanyard?' he replied.

I asked the other occupant of the vehicle to join his colleague which to my surprise, he did, although on reflection I feel he knew what was afoot. I then started to improve their education and understanding of military apparel. I informed them that it was not a 'lanyard' but a whistle cord as worn by those of the rank of sergeant and above in the Light Infantry. I also pointed out that the brassard on my right arm carried the badges of rank of sergeant, as worn by the LI.

I then informed them that I objected most strongly to their method of address which might be acceptable in the Royal Air Force but not with me. I took their names and numbers, as I felt inclined to report their behaviour.

I did nothing about the incident as I did not want to do anything that might delay my departure if it came about. I sometimes wonder if the lesson did anything to improve the two corporals' future handling of these situations, but I doubt it.

CHAPTER SEVENTEEN

Voila le commencement de la fin

Eventually, I was told to parade at the CO's office at 09:30 the next morning and I could attend in normal working dress, not my best gear. I guessed something had been heard concerning my possible return home.

I presented myself at the time specified and was told by the adjutant to enter the tent containing the CO's office. I entered, placed myself in front of the CO, saluted, then waited. The CO returned my salute, and went back to reading whatever he had been reading when I entered. After some moments he looked up. 'I'm afraid you posting to Strensall has been cancelled. A corporal from the KOYLI has got the job.'

Several moments' silence passed before he spoke again. 'However, all is not lost, as I am sending you back to the Depot prior to your going to the Recruiting Office in Hereford to spend your time recruiting until Boys have been enlisted in sufficient numbers for you to teach and train as you know what it is to be a Band Boy with its pitfalls.'

To say I was overwhelmed would be no exaggeration. It was

not every day such a posting was offered. However, when I'd calmed down, I realised what was afoot. I was being offered this posting in the hope that I would re-enlist, as my original enlistment had only months to run. I was dismissed and returned to the band, who were in rehearsal. I took my place among them and must have looked like the cat who'd got the cream as the BM asked me to step outside the tent while the band took a break. He asked me what the CO had said, and if I knew when I might be leaving. I was unable to give him any more details, other than I was being posted home.

Despite my impending move, duties still had to be carried out. I recall that the dance band, including me, had an engagement in an Officers' Mess in Naivasha. We went in the minibus that was used for educational visits. The dance band had used it before without any problems, in order to avoid the 'Curse of the 3-tonner'. Our journey took us along the Cigarette Road, so called because it had been constructed by Italian Prisoners of War during the 1940s who had received payment of three cigarettes a day. The road ran as straight as a die from the outskirts of Nairobi to Naivasha, a distance of some twenty miles following the undulating course of the Rift Valley's natural contours. In one of the dips one came across a small chapel built by the POWs. In fact it was so small it was difficult to get two persons inside at the same time, but what really attracted one's attention was a sign: 'Terrorists beware of Picnickers!' Who said there was no humour in the Emergency?

The dance went fairly well until we were asked if we would play for another couple of hours As it was already past midnight we declined which didn't go down well with the people running the dance. However we agreed to give them another hour, which seemed to pour oil on troubled waters. We were to learn later that this was far from the case, as they were very dissatisfied and made their feelings known to our company commander. A couple of days later he asked the BM, 'Couldn't the dance band have loosened up a bit and joined in the mood of the party?' I was pleased to hear that the answer he received was along the lines that the band were there to do a job not to be part of a three ring circus!

We finished the dance, packed up our instruments and music, rounded up our driver, loaded up and started on our way back to Nairobi. The road seemed to have an hypnotic effect on all of us but when the sun rose we realised just what hour it was. The driver started to nod over the driving wheel, so in order to keep him and ourselves awake we sang every song we could think of. About halfway, we came into a village where we could obtain some cold water and buy soft drinks, as well as stretch our legs in an attempt to get the blood flowing. It was during this stop we learned that the driver instead of getting his head down had indulged in a drinking bout with some of the waiters, also that he hadn't been to bed for two nights! We were not happy.

Eventually I received my orders to depart Kenya. I had been saying my farewells for some days so was pleased that I would at last be on my way, although it would take a few more days as I was destined to be a temporary resident in the local transit camp. Before I left the battalion I was asked to step into the band practice tent The band were all gathered there and one of the corporals who had been a Boy at the same time as me made a short speech before presenting me with a wonderful leather wallet embossed with a map of East Africa in the most beautiful colours. I kept the wallet for many years and have never handled such wonderful leather.

I was transported to the transit camp where I joined about twenty others awaiting passage home. While waiting we had to fill in passport applications as it seemed the Sudanese were not too happy about the passage of British troops through their country. We all had to have a photograph taken to be affixed to our passport forms. When we received our passport applications back for verification, I could not help but notice that the photograph attached to mine was not me. I raised this with the Warrant Officer in charge and was asked if I wanted to go home.

'Of course I do!'

'Then keep your head down and leave well alone!'

I doubt if I shall ever see Kenya again despite it becoming such a tourist attraction, but I was sorry to leave as we boarded the plane, along with a party of other military personnel, including a woman with babe in arms, who was very frightened as she had never flown before; she had to get to the UK as quickly as possible as her mother was seriously ill. As soon as we had taken off she became very frightened indeed and needed someone with her all the time. The cabin crew asked me if I would ask the men if they could help with issuing drinks and, if needed, looking after the baby.

As is the way with the British squaddie, every man took to the task without a grouse or grumble although one or two did show signs of embarrassment when it came to nursing the baby, not helped by the ribald remarks of their colleagues: 'What are you doing when we land, miss?'

A Medical Corps sergeant on board took over the duty of sitting with the mother as a source of comfort, while we assisted with tasks such as providing snacks and drinks to all the other passengers and the cabin crew provided whatever the baby and its mother required.

The captain of the aircraft radioed ahead so there would be a doctor to meet the plane when it landed for refuelling in

Malta. (We had by-passed Khartoum.) The plane was met on landing and a doctor came on board to examine the lady and suggested an injection to help calm her down. The lady agreed so while the rest of the passengers looked after the baby, the mother sat peacefully chatting with the other passengers for the remainder of the journey. However as we approached the UK we were informed that everywhere was closed in by a real 'pea souper' and the only airport open was Southend. Everyone's thoughts turned to the lady and her problem but we need not have worried as we learned she was to be met by an official car and transported to Blackbushe where her family were waiting to take her home, which was a short distance from there.

We all wished her well and set about the business of getting through customs. When it came to Passport Control the officials all had a laugh over the temporary documents and the photographs. We were informed that we need not have worried as the Sudanese only counted heads! Most of the passengers were continuing on by train to London, so after a refreshing cuppa, we were informed that our train was now at the platform and we should board as quickly as possible, because as a result of the fog, the train was running late.

On reaching London and leaving the station, I attempted to find a bus to Crystal Place as I wanted to spend a night at home before reporting in at the Depot. I was told that the buses had stopped running because of the fog, but if I hurried to the tube station I might just catch the last southbound train. Luckily the last train was running late because of the fog, so I was able to get as far as the Oval. On leaving the station I hailed a taxi who, after a lot of haggling, agreed to take me to my home address, despite the petrol rationing, provided I paid him a third more than was on the clock. I felt I was being swindled, but I wanted to get home and was in a fair mood.

After a reasonable sleep for the remainder of the night, I made my way to the Depot in Shrewsbury.

When I reported in to the Orderly Room, the first person I met was my old adversary from the NCOs' cadre in Germany, who was now Orderly Room Quarter Master Sergeant (ORQMS). The first thing he said was, 'Take those stripes down. You're not in the battalion now!'

I said nothing. At that moment the depot adjutant walked in and asked who I was, and upon being told, said to me, 'Come into my office, Sergeant.'

I followed him in and as soon as he got settled, he said, 'You are to be promoted with immediate effect to Acting Unpaid Sergeant,' then dismissed me with the words, 'Your posting to Hereford will be in orders in a couple of days.'

For the next couple of days I reported every morning but finding nothing for me, I wandered down into town, taking my leisure in one or other of the coffee bars, reading the papers or a book.

One day I decided to remain in my bunk and read a new book I'd bought. I must have found it really gripping as the first thing I knew was the door opening and the RSM entering. 'What are you doing still here?'

'I'm awaiting my posting order, Sir.'

'Come with me,' the RSM said.

Together we went to the Orderly Room where he asked one of the clerks, 'Have you anything for this sergeant?'

'I put the sergeant's movement order on the ORQMS's desk two days ago, Sir,' the clerk replied.

The RSM told me to disappear. My movement order was on Part Two Orders that evening!

I journeyed to Hereford by train where, at the station I wondered how I was going to get to the Drill Hall where I was to report to be taken on strength for such things as pay and general administration. I was still standing in the booking hall when a Royal Artillery sergeant entered and made some enquiry at the ticket office. As he was leaving I asked if he knew the best way to the Drill Hall. To my surprise he said he had a Land Rover outside, also that he was going to the Drill Hall and I was welcome to a lift. We travelled through Hereford and I looked out at all places I'd visited with my friend of Boys' Service days (now transferred to the Royal Army Pay Corps). On reaching the Drill Hall I started to unload my kit when the sergeant said, as he was in no hurry, he would wait for me while I reported in. I must admit at being surprised at this but thought no more about it.

Reporting in, I was directed to the office of the company commander, who turned out to be the ex-RQMS who had issued me with my stripes, whistle cord and sash, and who had since been commissioned. This officer informed me that although I came under his jurisdiction for admin, I would be billeted and mess with the Sergeants' Mess of the Boys Battery Royal Artillery at Bradbury Lines (later to be the home of the SAS). I began to get the impression that my new found colleague knew more than he had said, especially when I discovered that he was the local recruiter and I would be working from his office.

After getting settled in I made a tour of discovery. The sound of trumpets came drifting across the parade ground and I discovered the trumpet band at rehearsal. As I stood watching and listening I got into conversation with an adult 1/ bombardier and learned that all the trumpeters were volunteers and all practice was carried out in their own time. When I saw them in their full dress for the first time I could understand why they volunteered. They certainly looked the bees knees in their shell jackets, with all the lace and buttons, their skin-tight breeches, riding boots and fur busbies with plume and side red flash. The girls flocked around whenever they paraded.

I presented myself at the recruiting office in Commercial Road, wearing No.1Dress, as this was to be my working dress while I was in Hereford. My colleague was also dressed in No.1 Dress and I noticed that amongst his medal ribbons was one for the MBE.

It took many attempts to get him to disclose how he had won this award. It seems during the retreat to Dunkirk he had been taken prisoner but had managed to escape and while attempting to get back to this country had traversed quite a lot of occupied France. While doing this he had taken notes of many German positions and fortifications and one can imagine what would have been the penalty had he been caught with these notes in his possession.

Compared with the honours system of today, when sportsmen are receiving a similar award for actions that cannot be compared in any way, I sometimes wonder where we are going.

The recruiting office was in a converted shop which, by pure luck, had the original bay type windows left in, therefore we could stand behind the screen boards and had a magnificent view up and down the street, thus did not fall prey to visiting officers. The other very useful member of the staff was a cleaning lady who had a wonderful knack of being able to warn us of any likely visitors. How she did it I do not know but it certainly worked for us.

My colleague very often had to leave me in charge of the office. This was not too hard a task, especially if you remembered that Thursday was Market Day. On this day all the lads from all over the county came into Hereford to take the 'waters', and usually ended up in quite a state although some of them never showed all that much effect of the drink. One particular Thursday I was left in charge and there appeared in the office a character who said he wanted to re-enlist in the Parachute Regiment. He appeared to have had a drink but was not in a drunken state so I sat down with him and while talking took down some particulars for future use. I informed him that I would forward his details for consideration which seemed to satisfy him and he left. When I saw my colleague the next morning he burst out laughing. 'This man has indeed been in the Paras, but they don't want to know!'

It appeared he visited the office on a fairly regular basis, always received a polite refusal and was shown the door. It seemed I had a lot to learn about the recruiting business.

Part of my brief was to visit various brass bands and youth orchestras in the hope that some might like to continue their musical education in the Army. I must admit I took advantage of visiting bands in the London area to spend some time at home. It was while I was on a long weekend that the Commanding Officer of the Drill Hall rang both the office and Bradbury Lines demanding my immediate presence. On my return on the Tuesday I reported as requested and was told to pack my kit and report to Shrewsbury as I should have started my 'demob' leave the previous Thursday.

The truth was, I had enjoyed the past few months so much I had forgotten all about my pending discharge.

I returned to the Depot and again reported in to the Orderly Room to be greeted yet again by my old adversary in his usual sarcastic manner but I couldn't have cared less and ignored him as far as possible. The adjutant dealt with my documentation – discharge book and railway warrant to Woking (via London). After I had handed in all my kit except that which I stood up in I returned to the adjutant's office for my signature to be placed on my records for the last time. It was at this point I asked the adjutant if I could exchange my War Emergency driver's certificate for a 'pink slip', needed for me to obtain a civilian licence.

He looked a little taken aback at this request and said he was supposed to give me a driving test, but as I seemed a reliable person he would skip the test, with which he handed over the pink slip. So it is that other than the Advanced Drivers' examination and the DVLA Disabled test, I have never taken an official driving test.

I left Shrewsbury the next morning and made my way home as I wanted to make a fairly early start the following morning to Woking. Digs and I talked long and hard over the matter of my re-enlisting but in the end I made the decision not to re-enlist as I realised I now had the opportunity to start again, only this time with a wife and possibly a family in the future.

The next morning broke with a very bright sun and I felt fairly good as I made my way to the Demobilisation Centre in Woking. As you entered, you handed over your papers which were checked very thoroughly to make sure you were the person detailed. All being in order, you were passed along to a man with a tape measure who measured neck, waist, chest, inside leg and foot size. These details were entered on a form which was given to you and was requested at every stage of subsequent outfitting. One thing I noticed was that when you first started you were addressed by your rank but as you progressed the title, 'Mister' was used more often. My civilian issue consisted of:

Trilby, felt, grey   1

A SHROPSHIRE BOY

Raincoat, tan	1
Suit, light grey, consisting of	
Jacket, double-breasted	1
Trousers, pairs	2
Shirt, cotton, collarless	1
Collars, cotton	3
Studs, collar, back	1
Studs, collar, front	1
Cuff-links, pairs	1
Shoes, leather, black, prs.	1
Socks, cotton, black, prs.	2

All these items were packed into a brown cardboard box, tied with string and it seemed I was leaving the Army as I had enlisted, with an issue of clothing.

As I stood on the sun-soaked platform of Woking station with my cardboard box at my feet, I looked around at the sunny scene and, with a tinge of sadness, said to myself, 'What now?'

'What now' was not long in coming. I was offered and vetted to the highest degree for a job training as a 'watcher' in MI5. I was accepted and went on to spend fourteen years in that organisation.

But that's another story!

Aucto Splendore Resurgo
(Arise Again in Splendour)

A P Sisley

A SHROPSHIRE BOY

A P Sisley

A SHROPSHIRE BOY

A SHROPSHIRE BOY

A SHROPSHIRE BOY

A P Sisley

A SHROPSHIRE BOY

A SHROPSHIRE BOY